UNDERSTANDING THE CONSTITUTION

TEN THINGS EVERY CHRISTIAN SHOULD KNOW ABOUT THE SUPREME LAW OF THE LAND

Published by the Christian Law Association, P.O. Box 4010, Seminole, Florida 33775-4010.

www.christianlaw.org

Printed in the United States of America

CONTENTS

INTRODUCTION

The most important legal document in American history is the United States Constitution. It is the blueprint by which our government is to be operated. It is the guarantor, not the grantor, of our liberties. Yet, many Americans have never read this short document completely through even once, and most have an erroneous view of what it says!

In fact, a 2006 survey found that while 22% of Americans could name all five family members of the irreverent cartoon TV show *The Simpsons*, only one in 1,000 (one-tenth of one percent) could name all five of the freedoms guaranteed in the First Amendment. Only one in four Americans was able to name even one of these five important freedoms (freedom of speech, religion, press, assembly and petition for redress of grievances)!

When given a list of possible rights to choose from, the people surveyed did not do much better. One in five thought the right to own a pet was a protected First Amendment right! Thirty-eight percent believed the right against self incrimination was in the First Amendment (actually in the Fifth Amendment). These appalling results demonstrate a tragically widespread ignorance of our basic American freedoms.

This book is not intended to be a detailed legal analysis of the Constitution. It is intended to be a basic introduction to this most important of American documents, concentrating on those constitutional provisions that affect Christian liberty. For example, many Christians today believe that the Constitution requires the separation of church and state; yet, these words never appear in the Constitution or its amendments!

Every American, and especially every Christian American, should be aware of what the Constitution actually says. However, America as a nation can never be saved by the Constitution. America can only avoid God's judgment if Christians will heed the call of II Chronicles 7:14: *"If my people, which are called by my name, shall humble themselves, and pray, and seek my face, and turn from their wicked ways; then will I hear from heaven, and will forgive their sin, and will heal their land."*

Christians also have a Biblical duty to participate in their government and to pray for their elected leaders. I Timothy 2:1-4 states:

> *I exhort therefore, that, first of all, supplications, prayers, intercessions, and giving of thanks, be made for all men; For kings, and for all that are in authority; that we may lead a quiet and peaceable life in all godliness and honesty. For this is good and acceptable in the sight of God our Saviour; Who will have all men to be saved, and to come unto the knowledge of the truth.*

This passage of Scripture explains *why* we should pray. Our knowledge of our protected constitutional rights and duties will tell us for *what* we should pray.

As good citizens and good Christians, we should become very familiar with the laws of our nation. We are commanded in Scripture to obey the law. The Bible commands us to *"be subject unto the higher powers."* (Romans 13:1) In fact, I Peter 2:13-16 makes it quite clear that our submission to government is the will of God and an important aspect of our testimony:

> *Submit yourselves to every ordinance of man for the Lord's sake: whether it be to the king, as supreme; Or unto governors, as unto them that are sent by him for the punishment of evildoers, and for the praise of them that do well. For so is the will of God, that with well doing ye may put to silence the ignorance of foolish men: As free, and not using your liberty for a cloke of maliciousness, but as the servants of God.*

Yet, how can we obey the law or participate fully in our government if we do not know what the law actually says? This book is intended to be a blessing and an encouragement to Christians to learn more about the Constitution and its protection of our religious liberties.

The time may come when the religious liberties with which the Lord has blessed our nation will no longer exist in America, and Christians will be forced to decide whether to obey their government or to obey their Lord. Choosing to disobey government should always be a last resort, however, taken only after every attempt to reconcile man's law with God's law has failed. Until that time comes in a Christian's life, he is required by Scripture to submit even to despotic and immoral governments. When he has no other choice under God's laws but to disobey man's laws, his disobedience must be carried out within the narrow boundaries set by God.

The best guarantee that our constitutional freedoms will continue to be protected in America is to make certain that all citizens clearly understand both what those freedoms are and Who it is that has granted us those freedoms. After all, our government does not grant us freedom. God is the Grantor of freedom. Governments are only established by men, as our Declaration of Independence proclaims, to recognize and protect the freedom that has already been given to every person on the face of the earth by God Almighty, the Creator God of the Bible Who was recognized by all of America's Founding Fathers.

CHAPTER ONE

GOVERNMENT WAS GOD'S IDEA

> Government is an institution ordained and created by God for all eternity.

I. GOVERNMENT WAS ORDAINED BY GOD AS HIS DIVINE ORDER.

The concept of government is introduced in the very beginning of God's Word in the book of Genesis when God told Noah and his sons that a government of law would be established to protect the lives of men.

> *And surely your blood of your lives will I require; at the hand of every beast will I require it, and at the hand of man; at the hand of every man's brother will I require the life of man. Whoso sheddeth man's blood, by man shall his blood be shed: for in the image of God made he man.*
>
> *—Genesis 9:5-6*

Scripture makes it clear that God ordained government.

> *For there is no power but of God: the powers that be are ordained of God.*
>
> —*Romans 13:1b*

> *For by him were all things created, that are in heaven, and that are in earth, visible and invisible, whether they be thrones, or dominions, or principalities, or powers: all things were created by him, and for him.*
>
> —*Colossians 1:16*

Government is not something man invented, nor is there only one way for man to be governed. The Bible says nothing specifically about government being created "by the people, of the people, and for the people." Yet, God divinely established government as one of only three created institutions:

- ➤ The Home
- ➤ The Church
- ➤ The Government

Just as with the church and the home, when men speak about the government, they are speaking about an institution divinely ordained by God. Government is something very important and divinely ordained in God's Book and, whether good or bad, government must be respected as a God-created institution.

II. GOVERNMENTS ARE RAISED UP BY GOD.

Whether good or bad, there has never been, and never will be, a government that God does not raise up. God has total control in the affairs of the governments of this earth. *"By me kings reign, and princes decree justice. By me princes rule, and nobles, even all the judges of the earth."* (Proverbs 8:15-16)

Many examples exist in the Bible where God put into power rulers who loved and obeyed Him. (Psalm 2:6-7; Jeremiah 30:9; and Acts 13:21-22) Christians would love to see and should pray toward the end that only good men be placed in positions of power so they could take advantage of the Bible's promise that *"[w]hen the righteous are in authority, the people rejoice: but when the wicked beareth rule, the people mourn."* (Proverbs 29:2)

The Bible, however, contains just as many examples of God raising up wicked and unjust governments and using them to accomplish His purposes. God turns the most wicked and vile ruler's heart however He wants it. *"The king's heart is in the hand of the LORD, as the rivers of water: he turneth it whithersoever he will."* (Proverbs 21:1)

Sometimes God uses hostile powers to punish His people. (Jeremiah 51:11a) Other times He uses them to rescue His people. (Daniel 2:37, 38) At still other times, God uses wicked people to proclaim His salvation (John 19:10, 11) or to glorify His name. (Romans 9:17; Exodus 9:16) No ruler rises up unless and until God gives him the power and authority to do so. Thus, when Christians stand before a court or a state legislature, they are standing before an institution raised up by God, whether that arm of government is good or bad. Fortunately, in America, God has instituted a government in which Christians can play an important and active role.

III. GOVERNMENT IS SUSTAINED AND REMOVED AT GOD'S PLEASURE.

Governments succeed and fail according to God's good pleasure. When God ceases sustaining a government, that government is finished governing. Many Old Testament passages show how it pleased God to remove certain rulers.

The Book of Daniel describes how God removed Nebuchadnezzar, the King of Babylon, from power. Nebuchadnezzar was a vile man, vaunted in his imagination and almost unsurpassed in his wickedness. After he dreamed a troubling dream, he called Daniel to interpret it. Daniel reluctantly told Nebuchadnezzar that, although God had raised him to great power and authority, He was going to remove him from his position as king. For seven years, Nebuchadnezzar would go insane and live like an animal and then would be restored to the throne when he recognized that God, not the king, was in control.

> *This matter is by the decree of the watchers, and the demand by the word of the holy ones: to the intent that the living may know that the most High ruleth in the kingdom of men, and giveth it to whomsoever he will, and setteth up over it the basest of men.*
>
> *—Daniel 4:17*

The dream was fulfilled according to God's Word. Indeed, the king's sanity was restored to him when he blessed and praised God for His everlasting dominion and kingdom. Nebuchadnezzar finally declared,

> *And all the inhabitants of the earth are reputed as nothing: and he doeth according to his will in the army of heaven, and among the inhabitants of the earth: and none can stay his hand, or say unto him, What doest thou?*
>
> *—Daniel 4:35*

IV. CHRISTIANS WHO WANT TO OBEY GOD MUST OBEY GOVERNMENT.

Obedience to government is obedience to God. Conversely, to disobey government is to disobey God, which is a sin. Christians are to obey government because God commands it, not merely because they are politically conservative or patriotic or good citizens. Christians are not to obey only those governments that are just. Many people who are conservative or who love their country or who are good Americans are not necessarily obeying God.

In fact, Christians are not obedient to government because they are good citizens; Christians are good citizens because they are obedient to God.

Christians must not determine to obey only a just government because there will never be a truly just government until Jesus rules and reigns in eternity. Christians may only disobey that portion of the law that violates their faith, and they should always be careful to obey those portions of the law that do not violate their faith.

The obedient Christian should obey every part of the law that he can without actually violating his faith. A Christian's credibility is destroyed when an opponent proves in front of a judge and jury that most of the Christian's disobedience is not attached to his faith. Disobedience of laws for reasons unrelated to faith and conscience is disobedience to God Himself and could very well destroy the righteous stand being honorably taken by the Christian.

Fortunately, as Americans, we can still thank God for His blessing in raising up a good government for our nation. Not only is our government good, its foundational documents based our laws on the laws of God. It is a blessing to obey laws that are based on God's law.

CHAPTER TWO

THE DECLARATION OF INDEPENDENCE

> The Declaration of Independence, America's founding document, was based on God's laws.

In order to be effective citizens and to honor the government that God has graciously set over our nation, Christians must understand the Constitution and those documents that preceded it in America's history. The Declaration of Independence is the "why" of American government, while the Constitution is the "how." If looked at as a business corporation, the Declaration of Independence can be called America's Articles of Incorporation, while the Constitution can be seen as America's Bylaws. Just as with a business, the Bylaws may never legally contradict the Articles of Incorporation.

I. THE DECLARATION OF INDEPENDENCE ESTABLISHES THE BIBLICAL FOUNDATIONS FOR THE CONSTITUTION.

Many critics of Christianity's influence in America note that the Constitution does not mention God or the Bible. The truth is that it didn't need to because the Declaration of Independence had already declared twelve years earlier that its basic principles of freedom, justice, and dependence on God came from the Bible. The Constitution merely added to that foundational document the rules by which its founding principles would be put into practice. In 1897, the United States Supreme Court said:

> *The first official action of this nation declared the foundation of government in these words: "We hold these truths to be self-evident, that all men are created equal, that they are endowed by their Creator with certain unalienable rights, that among these are life, liberty, and the pursuit of happiness." While such declaration of principles may not have the force of organic law, or be made the basis of judicial decision as to the limits of right and duty, and while in all cases reference must be had to the organic law of the nation for such limits, yet the latter is but the body and the letter of which the former is the thought and the spirit, and it is always safe to read the letter of the constitution in the spirit of the Declaration of Independence.*
>
> *Gulf, C. & S. F. Ry. Co. v. Ellis*, 165 U.S. 150, 159 (1897).

II. THE LAWS OF NATURE AND OF NATURE'S GOD ARE THE BASIS FOR THE DECLARATION OF INDEPENDENCE.

In twenty-first century America the phrase *"the laws of nature and of nature's God"* is difficult to understand. As understood by the Founders, the laws of nature refer to God's unchanging principles established at Creation, while the laws of nature's God refer to the Bible. In declaring their independence from Great Britain and their dependence upon Providence, the authors of the Declaration stated:

> *WHEN in the Course of human Events, it becomes necessary for one People to dissolve the Political Bands which have connected them with another, and to assume among the Powers of the Earth, the separate and equal Station to which the Laws of Nature and of Nature's God entitle them, a decent Respect to the Opinions of Mankind requires that they should declare the causes which impel them to the Separation.*

We think of nature as mountains and trees and animals. We think of nature as describing the qualities of a person or thing. However, in the eighteenth century, when the Declaration of Independence was written, this phrase was understood to mean God's law, obtained through reason and science, and His law revealed to mankind in the Scriptures of the Old and New Testaments. America's Founding Fathers believed that God, as the Author and Judge of natural law, formed the basis in creation for our intuitions of right and wrong. They also believed that God is the context for our ability to reason and to govern ourselves. William Blackstone, the most popular expositor of law and government in America at the time the Declaration of Independence was written in 1776, expressed it this way:

> *Man, considered as a creature, must necessarily be subject to the laws of his creator, for he is entirely a dependent being. . . . as man depends absolutely upon his maker for every thing, it is necessary that he should in all points conform to his maker's will. This will of his maker is called the law of nature. . . . when [God] created man, and endued him with freewill to conduct himself in all parts of life, he laid down certain immutable laws of human nature, whereby that freewill is in some degree regulated and restrained, and gave him also the faculty of reason to discover the purport of those laws.*

> *This law of nature, being coeval[1] with mankind and dictated by God himself, is of course superior in obligation to any other— It is binding over all the globe in all countries, and at all times; no human laws are of any validity, if contrary to this: and such of them as are valid derive all their force, and all their authority, mediately[2] or immediately, from this original.*

---

[1] *Defined, "Originating or existing during the same period; lasting through the same era."*

[2] *Defined, "Acting through, involving, or dependent on an intervening agency. Being in a middle position."*

Upon these two foundations, the law of nature and the law of revelation, depend all human laws; that is to say, no human laws should be suffered to contradict these.

Thus, the "laws of nature" are God's unwritten laws implanted in man at the time of creation. They are God's general revelation in nature (see Romans 1:18-20). The laws of "nature's God" are His written laws revealed for us in Scripture.

III. THE SELF-EVIDENT TRUTHS ESPOUSED IN THE DECLARATION OF INDEPENDENCE ARE TRUTHS THAT ARE KNOWN INTUITIVELY BY ALL MANKIND AND DIRECTLY REVEALED IN SCRIPTURE.

The heavens declare the glory of God; and the firmament sheweth his handiwork.

—Psalm 19:1

The heavens declare his righteousness, and all the people see his glory.

—Psalm 97:6

In the Preamble to the Declaration of Independence, Thomas Jefferson spoke of *"self-evident truths:"*

WE hold these Truths to be self-evident, that all Men are created equal, that they are endowed by their Creator with certain unalienable Rights, that among these are Life, Liberty and the Pursuit of Happiness.

> *That to secure these Rights, Governments*
> *are instituted among Men, deriving their just*
> *Powers from the Consent of the Governed....*

In the Declaration's Preamble, Jefferson based America's government on those truths that are known intuitively by all men as revealed from God in the Bible—without the need for proof, discussion, or debate. For example, no discussion is needed to show that man is created in the image of God, black is not white, round is not square, and men are not angels. These are all facts of nature that cannot be proven; nevertheless, as human beings we are able to reason and see the truth of them.

IV. ONE IMPORTANT SELF-EVIDENT TRUTH IN THE DECLARATION OF INDEPENDENCE IS THAT ALL MEN ARE CREATED EQUAL.

Thomas Jefferson declared that one important self-evident truth for American government is that "*all Men are created equal.*" The truth of the equality of all men and women relates to humanity's equality in the sight of God. Before God all mankind has the same nature: we are all human; we are all sinful; we are all created in His image, and we are all loved by Him.

The word "equal" in the Declaration of Independence was not intended to mean that we will all achieve the same station in life or that we are all exactly the same in appearance, ability, assets, character, personality, or status. Instead, our equality before God and, therefore, our equality with respect to each other, preserves our unique creation as God's individual children.

V. MANKIND'S EQUALITY IS DEMONSTRATED IN HIS UNALIENABLE RIGHTS, WHICH ARE DERIVED FROM HIS RELATIONSHIP AND DUTIES TO THE CREATOR GOD.

Men are equal in the sense that God has created us all, male and female, with the same unalienable rights. Because we are created in God's image, we have a duty to respect and honor the rights or image of God in others. When others try to dishonor the image of God in us or in others, we have a duty to resist those efforts and to defend those God-given rights. The unalienable rights granted to Americans in the Declaration of Independence are rights which are based upon our corresponding duties owed to our Creator God.

Our God-given unalienable rights are sometimes called natural rights—those rights possessed by all mankind under the laws of nature in God's creation. As part of our birthright, these natural rights cannot be sold, given away, or taken from us. In fact, we cannot give them away even if we want to. Thus, we understand that God, not government, is the source of our rights. Government is responsible to identify and protect our rights, but government has no power to grant or deny them.

In declaring the endowment of our unalienable rights, Thomas Jefferson was clearly influenced by George Mason's Virginia Declaration of Rights, which said:

> *That all men are by nature equally free and independent and have certain inherent rights, of which, when they enter into a state of society, they cannot, by any compact,*

deprive or divest their posterity; namely, the enjoyment of life and liberty, with the means of acquiring and possessing property, and pursuing and obtaining happiness and safety.

VI. THE FIRST UNALIENABLE RIGHT IDENTIFIED IN THE DECLARATION OF INDEPENDENCE IS THE RIGHT TO LIFE.

The unalienable right to life is a gift from God that cannot rightfully be either surrendered or taken away. Our Declaration of Independence requires the government to protect this God-given right to life. Government may not take this right away from us or from our posterity.

When a right is unalienable, even the person who holds that right is not permitted to give it away. Therefore, our government must be accountable for protecting the unalienable right to life for all people regardless of their location, their quality of life, or their burden on other individuals or on society. William Blackstone said:

A man's limbs . . . are also the gift of the wise creator . . . . To these therefore he has a natural inherent right; and they cannot be wantonly destroyed or disabled without a manifest breach of civil liberty.

This first unalienable right is the basis for America's duty to respect and defend life created by God from conception through natural death. Our government has no authority to trample the unalienable right to life of the pre-born, of individuals with disabilities, of the elderly, or of any other person. All are equally precious in God's sight and created in His image. Therefore, the Declaration of Independence holds government accountable for securing the right to life for all people—no matter what their quality of life or station in society. Every life is created in the image of God. Government only acts lawfully when it equally protects the right to life of everyone under its authority.

VII.   THE UNALIENABLE RIGHT TO LIBERTY IN THE DECLARATION OF INDEPENDENCE IS NOT A RIGHT TO ENGAGE IN LICENSENTIOUS BEHAVIOR.

William Blackstone described man's unalienable right to liberty as one of God's gifts to man at creation. He described this liberty as consisting *"properly in a power of acting as one thinks fit, without any restraint or control, unless by the law of nature."* Algernon Sidney, another early expositor of government as instituted by God, saw liberty as an *"exemption from the dominion of any other. . . Man cannot be justly deprived of that liberty without cause."*

John Locke, a Christian enlightenment thinker, expressed it this way:

> *[T]hough this be a state of liberty, yet it is not a state of license. . . .[T]hat being all equal and independent, no one ought to harm another in his life, health, liberty or possessions; for men being all the workmanship of one omnipotent and infinitely wise Maker; all the servants of one sovereign Master, sent into the world by His*

> *order and about His business; they are His property, whose workmanship they are made to last during His, not one another's pleasure.*

William Blackstone taught that man's natural liberty has only two restraints. The first restraint is his duty to obey God and His laws. The second restraint is the restraint of a community, which a man freely accepts by choosing to live under a government and "*obliges himself to conform to those laws, which the community has thought proper to establish.*" Blackstone identified these community laws as "municipal laws," those which a government may choose to impose on its citizens to maintain order in those areas where God's law is indifferent.

VIII.   THE UNALIENABLE RIGHT TO THE PURSUIT OF HAPPINESS IS DERIVED FROM MANKIND'S DUTY TO LIVE ACCORDING TO THE MORAL LAWS OF GOD.

The unalienable right to the pursuit of happiness does not mean the right to happiness itself, but, rather, as George Mason believed, it is a right to the means to reach this happy condition. In recognizing this right, William Blackstone observed that individual happiness can only be attained by observing the laws of eternal justice and the unchanging moral laws of God. Aristotle had earlier observed that good character is the indispensable condition and chief determinant of happiness.

IX.   GOVERNMENT'S CHIEF PURPOSE IS TO SECURE MAN'S UNALIENABLE RIGHTS AS THEY HAVE BEEN BESTOWED BY GOD.

In America, our rights come from God, not from the state. Therefore, the state cannot take them away. What Uncle Sam gives, Uncle Sam can take away. But our nation's birth certificate, the Declaration of Independence, makes clear that our rights are unalienable because they come from God.

America's Founders and the authors of the Declaration of Independence believed that the purpose of government is to secure the unalienable rights of man. Conversely, the power of government is limited to protecting man's unalienable rights to life, liberty and the pursuit of happiness. To go beyond this mandate from God would mean the government was acting outside the boundaries of its just powers.

Thomas Jefferson incorporated the thinking of the greatest minds of his day into the Declaration of Independence when he said: *"Governments are instituted among Men."* By this he proclaimed that all men are free to live independently under the laws of nature or to live in a civil society. By choosing to live in a civil society, men authorize that society to make laws for them. As a result, governments derive *"their just Powers from the Consent of the Governed."* And the people freely agree to live under the authority of government. Algernon Sidney said:

> *[M]en could not resign their liberty, unless they naturally had it in themselves. Resignation is a public declaration of their assent to be governed by the person to whom*

*they resign; that is, they do by act constitute
him to be their governor.*

The central idea of the Declaration of
Independence—that the authority of government comes
from the people—was the ultimate implementation of a
revolutionary idea that had been developing in a practical
way over the previous 140 years as local Bible-based
commonwealths were established all along the American
seaboard. As John Winthrop, the first Governor of
Massachusetts, said: *"No common weale[3] can be founded
but by free consent."*

The Declaration of Independence was revolutionary
for people who had been governed by kings and queens for
thousands of years. In 1776, Thomas Jefferson adopted for
Americans an idea that had been stirring in the hearts of
enlightened Christian thinkers for hundreds of years when
he declared that King George III's authority to govern
came from God through the people, and that governing the
colonies was not the King's birthright. Once the American
people understood their equality, even with the King of
England, they were empowered through the Declaration of
Independence to withdraw their consent to his government
and to institute their own government independent of his
autocratic rule.

---

[3] *Or "commonwealth."*

X. IN DECLARING THEIR INDEPENDENCE FROM GREAT BRITAIN, AMERICANS UNDERSTOOD THAT THEY WERE MAKING THEMSELVES ENTIRELY DEPENDENT UPON THE PROVIDENTIAL CARE OF A SOVEREIGN CREATOR GOD.

Thomas Jefferson's climactic closing paragraph in the Declaration of Independence reflects the general sentiments of his day. He appealed *"to the Supreme Judge of the World,"* thereby recognizing that most people of his day believed in God and placed themselves under God's authority. He reinforced this view by closing the Declaration with these words:

> *And for the support of this Declaration, with a firm Reliance on the Protection of divine Providence, we mutually pledge to each other our Lives, our Fortunes, and our sacred Honor.*

In 1776, the American people understood the term divine Providence to mean God's providential care for and His control of the world. It was only their faith in God and their confidence that independence was His cause that gave the colonists, a ragtag bunch of patriots, the courage to pledge their lives, their fortunes and their sacred honor in declaring themselves to be free and independent of the greatest military power on earth at that time.

XI.   THE FIRST AND SECOND CONTINENTAL CONGRESSES ENDED WITH THE PUBLICATION OF THE DECLARATION OF INDEPENDENCE.

Samuel Adams of Massachusetts, the founder of the colonial Committees of Correspondence, the leader of the Boston Tea Party, and the last great Massachusetts Puritan, was the first person to call for the colonists to meet and discuss what to do about the oppression of the British king. The First Continental Congress assembled in Philadelphia in September 1774 to consider some options.

The colonies had become united through the First Great Awakening, a spiritual renewal sparked only a few years before by the revivalist preaching of George Whitefield and the conversion to Christ of a large percentage of colonial Americans. Their recently renewed faith united them in a way that would not have been possible earlier. King George III never imagined that the independent colonies would stick so closely together to oppose his unjust measures against them.

The First Continental Congress adjourned in October 1774 with plans to meet again the following spring. By the time the Second Continental Congress convened in May 1775, the colonists had tried every way they could think of to avoid war, but the British king was making peace impossible. With the battles of Lexington and Concord just a month earlier fresh on their minds, the delegates returned to Philadelphia.

By 1776, the delegates had begun the task of drafting their Declaration of Independence from Great Britain. During this era of American history, the Bible was the source most often quoted in political writings of the day.

America is the only country in the history of the world that was deliberately founded on the principles of the Bible. Around the time of the two hundredth birthday of America, *Time* magazine published an article called, "Looking to Its Roots," in which it recognized America's Biblical origins. The article said:

> *Ours is the only country deliberately founded on a good idea. That good idea combines a commitment to man's inalienable rights with the Calvinist belief in an ultimate moral right and sinful man's obligation to do good. These articles of faith, embodied in the Declaration of Independence and in the Constitution, literally govern our lives today.*

A few years earlier, *Newsweek* magazine had also featured a cover story discussing the Bible's impact on America. That article included these remarkable words:

> *[F]or centuries [the Bible] has exerted an unrivaled influence on American culture, politics and social life. Now historians are discovering that the Bible, perhaps even more than the Constitution, is our founding document: the source of the powerful myth of the United States as a special, sacred nation, a people called by God to establish a model society, a beacon to the world.*

And just how had these revolutionary Biblical ideas been promulgated among the ordinary citizens of the colonies prior to 1776? These Biblical principles of government had been taught to the people by the Black Regiment, the name assigned to the colony's preachers. While most of these men never donned a military uniform during the Revolutionary War, their black pulpit robes identified them as being just as important to the success of the Revolution as those who wore military uniforms.

Christianity indeed played a significant role in the development of our nation's birth certificate, the Declaration of Independence. An early American historian, Paul Johnson, wrote of this document:

> *There is no question that the Declaration of Independence was, to those who signed it, a religious as well as a secular act, and that the Revolutionary War had the approbation of divine providence. They had won it with God's blessing and, afterwards, they drew up their framework of government with God's blessing, just as in the 17th century the colonists had drawn up their Compacts and Charters and Orders and Instruments, with God peering over their shoulders.*

CHAPTER THREE

THE ARTICLES OF CONFEDERATION

> The Constitution was not the first statement of bylaws enacted by the newly free and united colonies.

In May of 1776, the Continental Congress assembled in Philadelphia determined to make provision for how a new government "of the people" would deal with the day-to-day problems of the national entity created by the Declaration of Independence. After a month of long consideration, on June 11, 1776, the delegates adopted a resolution to appoint a committee to determine the form their new confederation of colonies should take. One member from each colony was appointed to the committee.

The new governing document proposed by this committee on November 15, 1777, was called the Articles of Confederation. This document was put into printed form and sent to the legislatures of the thirteen colonies for their approval and ratification. The Articles were duly ratified by these legislatures on March 2, 1781, almost five years after independence from Britain was declared, but still two years before the colonies finally won the war against England.

I.   PROVISIONS OF THE ARTICLES OF CONFEDERATION.

The Articles of Confederation, under which the United States of America first operated, had no power of taxation, no power to regulate commerce, and no method of enforcing any measure passed by the national Congress with respect to all of the colonies. While there was a Congress composed of delegates from every colony in the union, there was no provision for an executive officer. The closest thing to a president was the presiding officer of Congress elected by his peers for one year. Congress itself was a single chamber body.

Under the Articles of Confederation, each state retained its independent sovereignty, and only those powers granted specifically to the United States could be exercised by the national Congress. Those powers primarily included mutual defense against common enemies and a general bond of mutual friendship and assistance with regard to the general welfare of all the states.

The Articles provided for mutual privileges and immunities for free citizens, free ingress and egress among the various states, free trade and commerce among the states, extradition of felons, full faith and credit to the acts of every other state, a means of resolution of property disputes between the states, regulation of common currency, weights and measures, a common administration of Indian affairs, and a common postal service. The

Congress appointed its own presiding officer, formed such committees as it deemed necessary, and raised needed military forces from the states that individually bore the cost of equipping them.

II.   THE ARTICLES OF CONFEDERATION ACKNOWLEDGED GOD.

Like virtually every early American document, the Articles of Confederation mentioned God, referring to Him as *"the Great Governor of the World."* The document ended with these words by which each signatory ratifying the Articles recognized the hand of God in raising up their new government:

> *And Whereas it hath pleased the Great Governor of the World to incline the hearts of the legislatures we respectively represent in Congress, to approve of, and to authorize us to ratify the said Articles of Confederation and perpetual Union.*

III.   THE ARTICLES OF CONFEDERATION BECAME INSUFFICIENT TO MEET THE NEEDS OF THE NEW UNITED STATES OF AMERICA.

While the Articles of Confederation saw the new union of states through the perils of the Revolutionary War, which ended in 1783, the document's structural flaws made it more and more unworkable over time. One such flaw was that every legislative measure had to be approved by all of the states; and getting all the states to agree unanimously on anything was very difficult.

Therefore, in May of 1785, two years after the successful conclusion of the War for Independence, a committee of the Congress issued a report recommending alterations to the Articles. The legislatures of the states were left to act on this recommendation. Rhode Island announced early on that it wanted nothing to do with any revision of the Articles and would refuse to approve any alterations. In fact, no delegates from Rhode Island attended the Constitutional Convention when it was finally organized.

Eventually, five states met and issued a report supportive of changes to the Articles of Confederation in the interests of the Union. These states called a meeting of all the colonies in May of 1786 in Philadelphia. The purpose of the meeting was to propose necessary changes in the Articles to the Congress. By 1787, seven states had convened and George Washington was unanimously elected to preside.

CHAPTER FOUR

THE CONSTITUTIONAL CONVENTION OF 1787

Drafting the new Constitution required the miraculous intervention of God.

The Convention that was called by the states in 1787 did not meet initially to draft a new Constitution. The stated purpose of this meeting was to revise the Articles of Confederation.

In February of 1787, the federal Congress accepted the suggestion of the interested states and adopted a resolution in favor of an assembly of all the states to consider the needs of the Union. This assembly was to develop and make plans and provisions adequate for the needs of the Union and to report their recommendations back to the Congress. Every state was invited to send delegates.

The vast majority of the fifty-five state delegates who attended the meeting in Philadelphia, later known as the Constitutional Convention, were professing Christians.

Only Benjamin Franklin and James Wilson of Pennsylvania were known to be Deists, while Hugh Williamson of North Carolina and James McClurg of Virginia may also have been non-Trinitarian. Historian John Eidsmoe concludes that, at most, 5.5% of those attending the Constitutional Convention were Deists (who believed in God, but did not believe in God's revelation or authority; and who believed that God created the world and its natural laws, but took no further part in its functioning). Most of the delegates had been educated in schools such as Princeton where theology and a serious study of the Bible were required subjects. Everyone who attended these schools, whatever their intended profession, received the same theological training as seminarians.

I.   THE CONVENTION OF 1787 SOON BECAME THE CONSTITUTIONAL CONVENTION.

When the colonial representatives first met in 1787 for what we now call the Constitutional Convention, they were not meeting for the purpose of drafting a brand new constitution. The Articles of Confederation, which had been written in 1777 and ratified in 1781, no longer seemed sufficient for the needs of the states. Alexander Hamilton said of the nation as it was being governed under the Articles of Confederation: *"In America . . . the government of the Union has gradually dwindled into a state of decay, approaching nearly to annihilation."*

Soon after the delegates began their attempt to revise the Articles of Confederation, Edmond Jennings Randolph, representing Virginia, stood up and proposed a complete overhaul of the Articles although, ironically, by the end of the Convention, he along with George Mason of

Virginia and two of the delegates from Massachusetts were the only delegates who chose not to sign the document.

To make a more workable government, the Constitutional Convention first decided to adopt the provision that it would take only nine of the thirteen states, essentially a two-thirds majority, for proposals to be enacted. This would be the same majority required for ratification of the new document itself. Nevertheless, even with only nine states required for agreement, the changes did not come easily.

II.   THE DELEGATES AGREED THAT THE FINAL DRAFTING OF THE NEW CONSTITUTION WAS A MIRACLE OF GOD.

Modern Americans tend to glamorize the writing of the Constitution; however, the process was anything but glamorous. The convention met at Independence Hall in Philadelphia between May and September of 1787. The weather was hot and muggy. The pace was slow going. Tempers flared. The delegates seemed to ramble in circles for weeks on end. Some delegates left—prematurely and permanently.

There was a great deal of acrimony in the early days of the convention, especially between the more populated states and the less populated states as they discussed how they should be represented in the new united government. There were also bitter conflicts over slavery as some, particularly in the North, loathed the practice, while others, particularly in the South, depended upon it for their economic viability.

In light of all the difficulties encountered in writing the Constitution, Alexander Hamilton reflected back years later about the Constitutional government that had emerged from this convention:

> *For my own part, I sincerely esteem it a system which, without the finger of God, never could have been suggested and agreed upon by such a diversity of interests.*

The Convention proceedings were so difficult that at one point, when Alexander Hamilton had left temporarily, George Washington wrote him a letter complaining about the whole enterprise:

> *I almost despair of seeing a favourable issue to the proceedings of the Convention, and do therefore repent [of] having had any agency in the business.*

The convention was deteriorating so badly that even Washington, its president, was beginning to regret being there! But when the delegates had finally agreed on a workable Constitution and the convention had adjourned, Washington described the outcome as miraculous:

> *It appears to me, then, little short of a miracle, that the Delegates from so many different States (which States you know are also different from each other in their manners, circumstances, and prejudices), should unite in forming a system of national Government, so little liable to well founded objections.*

James Madison also believed that a supernatural work of God had taken place at Independence Hall. He said:

> *The real wonder is that so many difficulties should have been surmounted, and surmounted with a unanimity almost as unprecedented as it must have been unexpected. It is impossible for any man of candor to reflect on this circumstance without partaking of the astonishment. It is impossible for the man of pious reflection not to perceive in it a finger of that Almighty hand which has been so frequently and signally extended to our relief in the critical stages of the revolution.*

James Madison, who is sometimes called "the Father of the Constitution," often spoke of what some call the "miracle in Philadelphia." His words are memorialized on the wall of the Madison Building in the Library of Congress in Washington, D.C.:

> *THE HAPPY UNION OF THESE STATES IS A WONDER; THEIR CONSTITUTION A MIRACLE; THEIR EXAMPLE THE HOPE OF LIBERTY THROUGHOUT THE WORLD.*

Historian and author Catherine Drinker Bowen described the atmosphere at the convention on June 9, 1787. The proceedings, which had begun in May, seemed to be going nowhere. *"At this point,"* she writes, *"and indeed throughout the month of June, one marvels the*

Convention did not dissolve and the members go home. The large states were if possible more stubborn than the small."

Progress was often slow going and discouraging. But men like George Mason were persistent. Mason, who ironically did not sign the final document, declared that he would *"bury his bones in Philadelphia rather than quit with no solution found."* By June 27, 1787, things had not improved. A Georgia delegate, William Few, described the morning of June 28 as *"an awful and critical moment. If the Convention had then adjourned, the dissolution of the union of the states seemed inevitable."*

But then the miracle happened. The following day there was a breakthrough. The great turning point of the Convention came on June 28, 1787, after weeks and weeks of frustratingly little progress, with a wonderfully moving speech made on the Convention floor. Benjamin Franklin, who gave that speech, was a Deist. He was not one of the vast majority of Christian delegates to the Convention who believed strongly in the God of the Bible. Nevertheless, Dr. Franklin made an impassioned speech, reminding his fellow delegates that God had always answered their prayers as a nation, even when they were at war. Now that things were going so badly, should they not again turn to the Lord for help? Besides, asked Franklin, how could they expect to successfully create a new nation without God's help?

Dr. Benjamin Franklin's words were recorded for posterity on that miraculous day:

Mr. President:

The small progress we have made after 4 or five weeks close attendance & continual reasonings with each other – our different sentiments on almost every question, several of the last producing as many noes as ays, is methinks a melancholy proof of the imperfection of the Human Understanding. We indeed seem to feel our own want of political wisdom, since we have been running about in search of it.

In this situation of this Assembly, groping as it were in the dark to find political truth, and scarce able to distinguish it when presented to us, how has it happened, Sir, that we have not hitherto once thought of humbly applying to the Father of lights to illuminate our understandings? In the beginning of the Contest with G. Britain, when we were sensible of danger we had daily prayer in this room for the divine protection – Our prayers, Sir, were heard, & they were graciously answered. All of us who were engaged in the struggle must have observed frequent instances of a superintending providence in our favor. To that kind providence we owe this happy opportunity of consulting in peace on the means of establishing our future national felicity. And have we now forgotten that powerful friend? or do we imagine we no longer need his assistance? I have lived, Sir, a long time, and the longer I live, the more convincing proofs I see of this truth – that God Governs in the affairs of men. And if a sparrow cannot fall to the ground without his notice, is it probable that an empire can rise without his aid? We have been assured, Sir, in the sacred writings, that "except the Lord build the House, they labor in vain that build it." [Psalm 127:1a] I firmly believe this; and I also believe that without his concurring aid we shall succeed in this political building no better than the Builders of Babel: We shall be divided by our little partial local interests; our projects will be confounded, and we ourselves shall become a reproach and bye word down to future ages. And what is worse, mankind may hereafter from this unfortunate instance, despair of establishing Governments by Human wisdom and leave it to chance, war and conquest.

I therefore beg leave to move – that henceforth prayers imploring the assistance of Heaven, and its blessing on our deliberations, be held in this Assembly every morning before we proceed to business, and that one or more of the Clergy of this City be requested to officiate in that Service.

Immediately after Dr. Franklin spoke, Roger Sherman of Connecticut seconded his motion for prayer. Many of those who saw and heard the oldest man among them make this earnest plea were deeply moved. New Jersey delegate Jonathan Dayton reported what he saw after Dr. Franklin's impassioned request for prayer:

The Doctor sat down; and never did I behold a countenance at once so dignified and delighted as was that of Washington at the close of the address; nor were the members of the convention generally less affected. The words of the venerable Franklin fell upon our ears with a weight and authority, even greater than we may suppose an oracle to have had in a Roman senate!

But there were others who had their own practical reasons for opposing the motion to begin each day with prayer. Dr. Franklin's motion for opening the sessions with prayer every morning was not acted upon because the Convention lacked funds to pay a clergyman, and also because the delegates were afraid that news of outside clergymen coming to assist in services would start rumors that dissension was breaking out in the Convention.

Edmund Jennings Randolph of Virginia proposed a compromise measure: *"That a sermon be preached at the request of the convention on the 4th of July, the anniversary of Independence; & thenceforward prayers be used in ye Convention every morning."* Benjamin Franklin himself seconded this substitute motion.

Within a week, on July 4, the entire assembly worshiped together at a nearby church in Philadelphia. While some difficulties continued to arise before the conclusion of the Convention's business in September, the delegates never returned to the fruitless acrimony that had existed prior to June 28.

Dr. Franklin's call for prayer played an important role in reminding the delegates at a critical time that without God's help all their efforts would be in vain.

On September 17, 1787, the final draft of the new Constitution was agreed upon. It was signed by most of the delegates and transmitted to Congress. From there, Congress forwarded the document to the legislatures of the thirteen states for approval and ratification. New York ratified the document on July 26, 1788, enabling the government to begin operating under the new Constitution on March 4, 1789.

This document included the seven original articles, but it did not include a Bill of Rights, something that had to be promised by Congress in order to have the document ratified by a sufficient number of states. The Bill of Rights, the first ten amendments to the Constitution, was proposed to the legislatures of the states on September 25, 1789. Virginia was the last state to ratify the new Constitution on December 15, 1791; however, approval from only nine of the thirteen states had been required for the document to be put into effect. North Carolina and Rhode Island also ratified the document after the first Congress went into session

The new federal government went into operation in 1789, with its temporary capital in New York City. The capital was moved to Philadelphia in 1790, and to Washington, D.C., in 1800.

CHAPTER FIVE

THE CONSTITUTION

The Constitution represents a compromise between those who desired a strong central, or federal, government and those who wanted to leave the greater power with individual states.

America's Founding Fathers who drafted the Constitution attempted to give the federal government enough power to carry out the functions intended, while permitting the states to retain enough power to safeguard the people from a tyrannical central government. Thus, the Constitution set up a system of checks and balances so that no one branch of the federal government could have absolute control. For example, the president could veto any act passed by both houses of Congress, but Congress could override a presidential veto. Likewise, the Supreme Court could declare an act of Congress to be unconstitutional, but only the executive branch was empowered to enforce a decision of the Supreme Court by force.

I. THE BIBLICAL UNDERSTANDING OF MAN'S SINFULNESS WAS THE GUIDING PRINCIPLE BEHIND THE CHECKS AND BALANCES IN THE UNITED STATES CONSTITUTION.

Even as our Founding Fathers were agonizing and compromising over the details of the Constitution, many of them recognized that something great was taking place among them. They were pursuing a course of action that had never before been pursued in all of human history. They were creating a document that would provide the newly independent colonies with self-government and freedom. Since then, the model they crafted has been admired and copied around the world. But before America could give the gift of self-government to the world, God gave the gift of freedom and self-government to America.

The Biblical understanding of the sinfulness of man was the guiding principle behind the United States Constitution. The framers of the Constitution drew their inspiration from the Bible. They intended for America to be one nation under God. They had no intention of establishing an agnostic or atheistic state.

James Madison played an especially significant role in shaping the American Constitution. While some claim it is an exaggeration, others have called him the father of the Constitution or its chief architect. Whatever view one adopts, there is no question that Madison's influence in helping to frame the new government was invaluable. And Madison's view of government and law had been shaped primarily by his Biblical Christianity.

As a Virginian, Madison would have been expected to study at the Anglican College of William and Mary. Instead, he chose to attend the College of New Jersey (now called Princeton) where he sat under the direct tutelage of Dr. John Witherspoon, a prominent Bible-believing patriot who later became the only minister to sign the Declaration of Independence. During Madison's stay at Princeton, a great revival took place, and it was believed that he was a participant in that revival. Contemporary historians report that on Madison's return to Virginia from Princeton, he began to conduct worship services in his father's house. When he announced his candidacy for the Virginia Legislature, his opponents objected, saying that he was better suited for the pulpit than for the legislature.

Perhaps the most important lesson Madison learned from his Princeton education was his firm belief in the Biblical doctrine of man's inherent sinfulness. Because of man's sin, he believed that government must institute a rigorous system of checks and balances to protect its citizens from tyranny. His concept of checks and balances took into account the temptation in man's nature to greed and selfishness. It withdrew from any one man, or from any group of men, the power to become tyrannical. In 1787, Madison wrote:

> *All men having power ought to be distrusted to a certain degree.*

James Madison was not alone among the Founders in professing the Christian doctrine of original sin and insisting that this theological concept be incorporated into the new government through an elaborate system of checks and balances. The Founding Fathers all knew that because man was sinful, power could not be vested in any one person.

Even Benjamin Franklin, who generally claimed not to place faith in the Bible, recognized man's natural propensity toward despotism when he said: *"There is scarce a king in a hundred who would not, if he could, follow the example of Pharaoh, get first all the people's money, then all their lands, and then make them and their children servants forever."*

II. A SECTION BY SECTION ANALYSIS OF THE CONSTITUTION

The Constitution consists of seven articles setting up the government of the United States of America. The text of the Constitution has, by and large, remained unchanged for more than two hundred years, although the interpretation of that text by the courts has changed drastically over time. This chapter presents an overview of the key provisions and a brief commentary on each article. (See Appendix 1 for a complete copy of the original Constitution.)

A. The Preamble

We the people of the United States, in order to form a more perfect Union, establish justice, insure domestic Tranquility, provide for the common defense, promote the General Welfare, and secure the Blessings of Liberty, to ourselves and our Posterity, do ordain and establish this Constitution for the United States of America.

The Preamble to the Constitution is not law; it is merely a declaration of the intent and purpose of the document. It implies that the union has already been ongoing and that this document is intended to perfect that ongoing union. In fact, the Constitution is dated in the twelfth year of the independent existence of the United States, a date that harkens back to the Declaration of Independence. This date demonstrates the Constitution's incorporation of the foundational principles in that earlier document, which were based on a recognition of the natural and revealed laws of a Sovereign Creator God.

When the Preamble states that the Constitution is designed to *"secure the Blessings of Liberty,"* it recognizes a key principle of the Declaration of Independence—that those "Blessings" are bestowed by God and are only recognized and secured by the state.

> *By calling the advantages of liberty "blessings," the Constitution...nonetheless, in its understanding of the connection between happiness and virtue, aligns itself decisively with traditional moral philosophy and moral theology.*
>
> —Jaffa, Harry V., *The American Founding as the Best Regime: The Bonding of Civil and Religious Liberty.* The Claremont Institute, 1990,1997.

B.   Article I: The Legislature

The legislature is the first branch of government discussed in the Constitution. This placement attests to the prominence assigned by the Founders to the representatives of the people elected in each state.

Congress alone, as stipulated by the Constitution, possesses the exclusive responsibility and authority to determine the need for and to enact binding laws for the nation. Article I reflects the overarching revolutionary American concept that the people, through an elected legislature, are sovereign, not a monarch or an elite ruling body. Although legislation may be recommended by the executive branch of government, or even by individual citizens or groups of citizens, the responsibility for enacting legislation rests exclusively with the legislative branch. The legislative branch also has the power to set the scope and jurisdiction of the judicial branch of government, with the exceptions of those specific enumerations of power listed in Article III.

Although Congress may not grant legislative power to the executive branch of government, Congress today delegates a great deal of regulatory authority to certain executive agencies, which has the force of administrative law. While such regulations must be compatible with the Constitution, such regulatory administrative laws are more numerous today than was likely anticipated by the Founders. Congressional authority to act under the Constitution can be divided into two categories: enumerated powers and implied powers.

Enumerated powers are certain particular endowments of power specifically given to Congress under the Constitution. For instance, all legislative powers granted within the Constitution were vested in Congress. Along with the authorization to make laws, the Constitution also gives Congress other specific authorizations to act.

At the head of list of powers given to the Congress was the power to uniformly *"lay and collect Taxes, Duties, Imposts and Excises, to pay the Debts and provide for the common Defence and general Welfare of the United States."* Other enumerations set forth in section 8 include the power to do the following:

1. Borrow money on the credit of the U.S.;

2. Regulate commerce with foreign nations;

3. Establish uniform laws on naturalization and bankruptcy;

4. Coin money and fix the standard of weights and measures;

5. Provide for the punishment of counterfeiting the securities and current coin of the U.S.;

6. Establish post offices and post roads;

7. Promote the progress of science and useful arts through copyright, patents and trademarks;

8. Constitute tribunals inferior to the Supreme Court;

9. Define and punish piracies and felonies committed on the high seas, and offenses against the Law of Nations;

10. Declare war, grant letters of marque and reprisal, and make rules concerning captures on land and water;

11. Raise and support an army;

12. Provide and maintain a navy;

13.   Make rules for the government and regulation of the land and naval forces;

14.   Provide for calling forth the militia to execute the laws of the Union, suppress insurrections and repel invasions;

15.   Provide for organizing, arming, and disciplining the militia, and for governing any part of them as may be employed in the service of the United States;

16.   Exercise exclusive legislation in all cases whatsoever, over the District of Columbia and all places purchased by the consent of the legislature for forts, magazines, arsenals, etc.; and

17.   Make all laws which are necessary and proper for the carrying into execution of the enumerated powers, and all other powers vested by the Constitution in the Government of the United States.

Implied powers are powers not specifically enumerated in the Constitution, yet still capable of receiving constitutional protection. These implied powers of Congress encompass the right of Congress to do whatever is "necessary and proper" to enact the legislation it passes. These parameters are broadly set and widely interpreted, giving our modern Congress much discretion to act freely as it legislates.

The Constitution gives explicit instructions for the organization of a bicameral legislature. Pursuant to the Constitution, Congress is to be made up of two houses—the House of Representatives and the Senate.

1. Article I: section 2: The House of Representatives

In the House of Representatives, the number of congressional delegates is determined by each state's population. Following a national census every ten years, the number of representatives assigned to each state is reapportioned.

In order for a person to qualify to take office, he or she must be at least twenty-five years old and must have been a United States citizen for at least seven years. This requirement that a House member must have been a citizen for seven years is further proof that the Constitution recognized the union had already been in existence prior to the ratification of the Constitution and, therefore, incorporated the provisions of the Declaration of Independence.

The requirements for serving in the House, particularly the age provision, have not always been followed closely. For example, the youngest person to ever serve in the House was William Claiborne of Tennessee, who was only twenty-two years old, and was seated by a special resolution of the House. The Constitution also stipulates that House members are to be re-elected by the people every two years.

The House of Representatives chooses its own Speaker and other officers. The House has the sole power of impeachment of a President or of members of the federal judiciary.

2.   Article I: section 3: The Senate

The Senate is comprised of two delegates from each state, no matter how large or small. Originally, senators were chosen by the various state legislatures, not by a vote of the general population of the state. Since 1913, with the adoption of the Seventeenth Amendment, Senators have been elected by all the citizens of each state in a popular election.

To qualify as a senatorial candidate, a person must be at least thirty years of age and a citizen of the United States for at least nine years. However, as with the House, the youngest person ever to serve in the Senate was John Eaton in 1818, who was only twenty-eight years old. In more recent times, Senator Rush Holt of West Virginia was only twenty-nine years of age when he was elected in 1935. It was determined at that time that he could not be sworn in until he reached his thirtieth birthday.

The Senate also chooses its own officers, with the exception that the vice president shall serve as the president of the Senate. The vice president has no vote in the Senate unless that body is equally divided, in which case the vice president casts the deciding vote.

The Constitution divides certain powers and procedures that are specific to only one house of Congress. This is part of an internal system of legislative checks and balances. For example, while the House of Representatives has the sole power of impeachment of the president, federal judges, or justices of the Supreme Court, the Senate is given the "sole Power to try all impeachments." As seen in recent history with President Bill Clinton, the two legislative bodies do not always agree. The House impeached the forty-second president, but the Senate refused to remove him from office.

After the House has impeached a president, the Senate sits under oath to conduct an impeachment trial with the Chief Justice of the Supreme Court designated to preside over the trial. In cases of impeachment, if found guilty, judgment is limited to removal from office and disqualification to hold any future elective or appointed office in the United States. A conviction or lack thereof by Congress, however, does not disqualify that person from being indicted or tried later in the proper court and from being punished as the laws which were broken provide. In President Clinton's case, although not found guilty and removed from office by the Senate, he was later punished for his perjury and obstruction of justice by having his bar license suspended in Arkansas, the state in which he was licensed to practice law.

3. Article I: section 4: Elections

While Congress may at any time enact laws to control certain aspects of elections, the Constitution grants to state legislatures the power to control the dates, times, and manner of conducting and certifying elections. The manner in which the state of Florida chose to certify its election became an issue in the presidential election of 2000, and the United States Supreme Court eventually permitted Florida's certification for President George W. Bush.

This section requires that the Congress meet at least once during every year. When the Congress goes into recess, any bills passed during that time must be signed by the president within ten days, Sundays excepted (another reflection of the Christian roots of the Constitution). If the president does not sign a bill within ten days, it is not enacted and is considered to be a pocket veto. While the Congress is in session, it may override a presidential veto by a super majority in both chambers.

4. Article I: section 5: Rules of Procedure

Both the House and Senate are given the right to determine their own rules of operation. They may by subpoena compel witnesses to appear and testify before them and may hold in contempt any witnesses who do not appear or do not answer questions. Such witnesses may also be found guilty of perjury for giving false testimony under oath. Congress does not have any power to punish those found guilty. The House and Senate, however, do have the power to punish their own members for unseemly behavior or misconduct, a power which extends to imprisonment. A two-thirds majority of each chamber may also expel a member.

The Constitution requires legislative bodies to keep records of their deliberations and to publish these records, with the exception of any matters requiring secrecy. This *Congressional Record* is available to any interested citizen. Votes of Congress members, however, are not recorded unless one-fifth of the members request that the votes be entered in the printed record.

5. Article I: section 6: Compensation

Members of Congress are compensated for their service, interestingly, at a rate which they themselves determine. One of the privileges of office includes immunity from arrest while attending a legislative session or while traveling to or from such sessions, except for offenses of treason, felony, or breach of the peace. Except for actual charges of liable, Congress members are immune from liability while performing their duties of office. Congress members may not simultaneously serve in other government offices, including appointive offices or the military, during their term of service in the Congress.

6.   Article I: section 7: Revenue Bills

While the Senate may propose or concur with amendments as with other bills, only the House of Representatives may propose bills for raising revenues (taxes). This provision does not prevent the Senate from amending revenue bills, however.

When a bill has passed in both legislative chambers, it is sent to the president who must either sign or veto it (including pocket vetoes). If he vetoes a bill, he must return the bill to the legislature, stating his objections, whereupon the bill may be reconsidered and passed without the president's signature by a two-thirds majority of the membership present in both chambers. If the president does not sign the bill or return it to the Congress with his objections, the bill is enacted without his signature (except in the case of a pocket veto in which case the bill dies without his signature after ten days). There are a few exceptions to this ten-day rule, when only one chamber is in session or when the president is out of the country. The date on which the president signs the bill or both chambers override the president's veto, or the day designated in the bill itself, is the date on which that bill becomes law.

7.   Article I: section 8: Enumerated Powers

The enumerated powers of the legislature were listed beginning on page 47.   Taxes include duties on imported goods, excises on utilities, consumption taxes on goods and services, and income taxes which were later authorized by the Sixteenth Amendment. Tax money must be used for the common defense or general welfare of the United States, provisions which have become very broadly interpreted. Courts have held that the collection of taxes is not subject to due process under the Fifth Amendment because of the need for government to collect the revenues needed to operate. The government may seize personal property and may even ignore complaints about the validity of the taxes assessed. An act of Congress for the general welfare must be effective for the entire nation and may not be specific to a particular area; however, certain local projects are determined to be good for the overall general welfare of the United States, establishing the precedent for what is often called "pork barrel" legislation, benefiting particular congressional districts.

Congress may borrow money, a power it has delegated to the Federal Reserve System, which now has complete control of currency in the United States.   The Congress may also regulate international and interstate commerce, a power which has also been broadly interpreted. Courts have interpreted the commerce clause to enable Congress to influence any activity that might have a reasonably substantial national impact on commerce. Courts have held relatively few areas to be outside of Congress's commerce authority.

Congress has power over uniform bankruptcy laws and over naturalization of aliens and immigrants. It has the power to coin money, a power which is also delegated to the Federal Reserve. Congress has the power to uniformly punish counterfeiting and the power to fix the standards of weights and measurements in a uniform manner.

Congress has delegated to itself very broad powers under its regulation of the postal system. Congress has power over patents and copyrights and power to define and punish piracies and felonies on the high seas.

Another power of Congress is the power to constitute federal judicial tribunals below the level of the Supreme Court, to which powers are enumerated in Article III. Congress has the power to grant or restrict the jurisdiction of lower federal courts and of the U.S. Supreme Court where jurisdiction is not specifically enumerated in Article III. However, Congress may not exercise this power in a manner that would violate the due process rights of citizens under the Fifth Amendment.

Congress has the power to declare war, to declare an end to war, and to raise and support armies and other military forces, including the National Guard. Congress may seize enemy property within the United States, while its own citizens' due process rights must be respected except for the most imminent dangers. Congress has the power to acquire and administer property within the boundaries of the various states. This includes park areas, wildlife refuge areas, and forestry preserves.

Another broad power granted to the Congress is the power to enact "all necessary and proper" laws for executing its enumerated powers. These are the "implied" powers of Congress and grant a very broad discretion to the legislature. Congressional laws may be challenged in federal courts as being unconstitutional.

8. Article I: section 9: Prohibited Powers

The specific provision in the first clause of this section was included as a compromise in order to achieve agreement on the Constitution between the northern states who wanted to eliminate slavery and the southern states that believed slavery was essential to their economy. This clause granted the South a twenty-year reprieve in its conduct of the slave trade; however, in deference to the North, it prohibited the importation of slaves into the United States after the year 1808.

Other items covered in this section include the provision of a judicial *habeas corpus* ("to have the body") in cases where there is a question as to the legitimacy of detaining persons. A writ of *habeas corpus* requires a judicial review of circumstances surrounding a person's imprisonment or restraint. Bills of Attainder (punishment without benefit of trial) and *ex post facto* laws (punishment for acts committed before legislation to make them crimes) are prohibited since these could annul individual rights.

Other provisions prohibit titles of nobility, which would grant certain individuals favored treatment. Certain powers are denied to states, such as the power to enter into foreign treaties, to levy taxes on exports from the state, to tax individuals based on a head tax or census count (with the exception granted later in the Sixteenth Amendment for the income tax).

C.   Article II: The Executive Branch

The executive power under the Constitution is vested in the president, who holds office for a term of four years. Although President Franklin D. Roosevelt, was elected to four terms in office, the Twenty-third Amendment now limits presidents to two terms in office. Executive powers are broad, including regulatory powers granted to the executive by the legislature and the power to issue Executive Orders which have the force of law. The basic constitutional duties of the president, however, are to see that the acts of the Congress are properly and faithfully administered.

1.   Article II, section 1: Electoral College, Qualifications, Succession, etc.

Unlike members of Congress, the president is not elected to office by the popular vote of the people. In fact, several times in our nation's history the candidate receiving the greatest number of popular votes has failed to win in the Electoral College:

> ➤ In 1824, Andrew Jackson received more popular votes than John Quincy Adams.

> ➤ In 1876, Samuel J. Tilden received more votes than Rutherford B. Hayes.

> ➤ In 1888, Grover Cleveland received more votes than Benjamin Harrison.

➤ In 2000, Al Gore received more popular votes than George W. Bush, who received the most votes in the Electoral College.

Instead of deciding the presidential election by popular vote, each state selects a number of electors, equal to the number of senators and representatives for the state. The electors then meet and cast their ballots, which are certified according to the rules and procedures of each individual state. This process is known as the Electoral College. Use of the Electoral College levels the playing field for voters in large and small states and in urban and rural areas. If elections were decided based only on the popular vote, more populous states and large cities would have greater power to elect a president. Candidates might completely avoid campaigning in less populated states and rural areas.

The candidate receiving the greatest number of votes in the Electoral College, *"if such Number be a Majority of the whole Number of Electors appointed,"* becomes president. There have been two times in our nation's history when the Electoral College has failed to reach a majority. In such cases, the election is decided by the House of Representatives.

➤ In 1800, Thomas Jefferson and Aaron Burr each received seventy-three electoral votes. The House chose Jefferson to be president.

➤ In 1824, John Quincy Adams received eighty-four electoral votes, and Andrew Jackson received ninety-nine. Even though Jackson had the most electoral votes, he did not have a majority "of the whole Number of Electors appointed," so the vote went to the House, which selected Adams.

In the 2000 election, had the candidates not taken the controversy over the certification of votes in Florida to the United States Supreme Court, the election might have gone to the House of Representatives, controlled at that time by the Republicans, which would most likely have selected George W. Bush over Al Gore.

To qualify as a presidential candidate, a person must be at least thirty-five years of age, a natural born citizen, and a resident of the United States for at least fourteen years. This section also sets the succession to the office of president either through death or removal. It also sets the president's compensation, which must remain fixed during his term in office, and provides for the president's oath of office.

2.   Article II, section 2: Powers

The enumerated presidential powers include the power to be Commander in Chief of the military forces; the power to grant reprieves and pardons for offenses against the United States in all cases except impeachment; the power to make treaties with the advice and consent of the Senate; and the power to nominate, and with the Senate's advice and consent, to appoint ambassadors, judges, and all other officers of the United States whose appointments are not otherwise provided for by the Constitution.

3.   Article II, section 3: Recess Powers

The president's powers include the power to fill vacancies during legislative recesses (such as recess appointments of judges or executive officers). These appointments must expire no later than the end of the next session of the Senate. The president is required to provide the Congress with a State of the Union message, which for much of our nation's history was given in writing rather than orally. The president also has the power to recommend legislation, convene or adjourn the legislature in an emergency, conduct foreign diplomacy, and issue commissions for military officers.

4.   Article II, section 4: Removal from Office

The president or vice president may be impeached and removed from office upon conviction by the Senate of treason, bribery, or other high crimes and misdemeanors. These terms are not specifically defined; however, generally a high crime is considered to be a felony, while a misdemeanor is a lesser crime.

D.   Article III: The Judiciary

The federal court system derives its power from Article III, which provides for one Supreme Court and *"such Inferior courts as the Congress may from time to time ordain and establish."* Our current federal court system consists of three levels: district courts, circuit courts, and the Supreme Court.   In addition, there are several specialized courts, such as tax courts, admiralty courts, bankruptcy courts, etc.   The nine Justices of the

Supreme Court and the judges of inferior federal courts are appointed to office and serve for life, unless impeached.

There have not always been nine members serving on the Supreme Court. At America's founding, there were only five Supreme Court Justices. During the presidency of Franklin D. Roosevelt, the number of Justices serving on the Court was increased, no doubt to gain a majority of votes to insure that the president's New Deal legislation would be upheld. This action was described at the time as "packing the court."

As with the other two branches of government, the judicial powers are specifically enumerated. The federal judiciary has limited jurisdiction to hear cases. The specific parameters of federal jurisdiction include all cases arising from the following: the Constitution; the laws of the United States; treaties; cases involving ambassadors; cases of admiralty and maritime law; whenever the United States is a party; and, controversies between two or more states or their citizens. Additional jurisdiction may be granted or withheld by the Congress. Congress is granted the constitutional authority to establish or abolish lower federal courts and to determine their jurisdiction.

All federal judges, who are appointed by the president with the consent of the Senate, serve for life unless impeached. Their compensation may not be lowered during their time in office.

Because the Court was given no power to enforce its decisions, most of the Founding Fathers never envisioned the possibility of a Supreme Court that could become an elite ruling oligarchy. One important exception was Thomas Jefferson who feared the Court could eventually claim too much power. The executive branch was given the power of the sword, while the legislative branch was given the power of the purse. The only power foreseen by most for the judicial branch was the power of persuasion and of deciding specific legal cases as they arose.

Article III also defines the term "treason," which exists only when war is levied against the United States, or when aid and comfort is given to an enemy of the United States. The limitations of this definition allow the federal judiciary to hear cases coming within the constitutional definition but simultaneously to act as a safeguard to prohibit legislative or judicial creation of new treasons for which punishment could be rendered.

E.   Article IV: Relations Between the States

Regulating peaceful relations between the states is an important function of the judiciary, as well as of the legislature.

1.   Article IV, section 1: Full Faith and Credit

The Constitution requires that full faith and credit be given in each state to *"the public Acts, Records, and judicial Proceedings of every other State."* This means that each state must recognize the laws of the other states, although one state is not required to enforce the laws of another state. For example, most states do not recognize common law marriages. In the past, a common law marriage generally occurred when a man and woman lived together, holding themselves out to the public as husband and wife, for a specified period of time. However, if the couple moved to another state and their common law marriage was legitimate in the state in which the couple lived previously, the new state of residence was required to recognize the marriage, even in contravention of its own law. To do otherwise would create chaos.

Another example of interstate full faith and credit can be found in the recent same-sex civil union and marriage controversy. Since the states of Vermont and Massachusetts legalized various forms of same-sex civil unions, other states will have difficulty under the full faith and credit doctrine of the Constitution in not recognizing these unions, despite the fact that a great many of the states have passed state Defense of Marriage Acts (DOMAs).

The full faith and credit doctrine, while preventing chaos and establishing uniformity among the states, is a dangerous constitutional doctrine when society's morals begin to slip in one portion of the nation, because other states are then forced to follow suit and lower their own moral standards. When one or two states began to recognize "quickie" divorce and remarriage in the mid-twentieth century, for instance, other states with higher standards were forced by the courts to recognize these marriage dissolutions.

Today the issue being forced on states is the issue of "same-sex marriage." This is the reason why passage of a Federal Marriage Amendment defining marriage as between one man and one woman has become critical for a majority of states that continue to outlaw same-sex marriage or unions. As long as America followed the common law, it was understood that our laws were based on the laws of God; therefore, it was not necessary to define marriage. Since 1938 when the Supreme Court abolished the common law in the United States (*Erie v. Thompkins,* 304 U.S. 64), all our laws are now statutory laws or executive orders. Therefore, the possibility exists for marriage to be statutorily or judicially defined in an immoral and ungodly manner that could not have been imagined even a few years ago.

2.   Article IV, section 2: Privileges and Immunities

The citizens of each state *"shall be entitled to all Privileges and Immunities of Citizens in the several States."* This section provides for extradition of accused criminals from one state back to the state in which the crime was committed, except that these provisions were abolished with reference to the return of slaves when slavery was abolished in the United States after the Civil War by the Thirteenth Amendment.

3.   Article IV, section 3: Admission of New States

New states can be admitted into the union only under the following conditions: (1) no new state can be formed or erected within the jurisdiction of any other state; and (2) no state may be formed by the joining of two or more states, or parts of states, unless the particular state's legislature and the United States Congress consent. New states have been regularly admitted into the union, with the last being Alaska and Hawaii, which have no common borders with the continental states. Puerto Rico has also from time to time considered statehood, but to date has not voted to join the union.

The Constitution provides for the federal government to acquire and dispose of property, whether outside of the territorial United States or from within the several states. Article IV also guarantees the right of states to choose their own officers, to make their own laws, and to be protected by the federal government from invasion.

F.   Article V: Amending the Constitution

The Founding Fathers realized that the Constitution would not address all future issues that might arise. Therefore, if the new nation were to survive and flourish, there had to be a formal means of amending the Constitution. The Founders provided two avenues for amending this document, neither going through the executive branch or the judiciary. These methods are as follows: (1) by congressional and state approval; and (2) by means of a constitutional convention.

Whenever two-thirds of both houses deem it necessary, Congress may propose amendments to the Constitution. Amendments proposed under this procedure are only valid after ratification by three-fourths of the states' legislatures. The fact that Congress proposes an amendment does not ensure its approval.

If two-thirds of the states' legislatures request it, Congress may call a constitutional convention. Any Constitutional amendments proposed under this procedure are valid only when ratified by separate conventions in three-fourths of the states' legislatures.

G.   Article VI: The Supremacy Clause and Oaths

The Constitution and the laws passed by Congress are the supreme law of the land; and federal law will control whenever federal and state laws conflict. This Article also provided for the assumption of debts entered into during the twelve years prior to the ratification of the Constitution (a provision also recognizing the previous existence of the union since the Declaration of Independence).

Article VI requires all U.S. Senators and Representatives, and *"all executive and judicial Officers, both of the United States and of the several States,"* to be bound *"by Oath or Affirmation to support this Constitution."*

Anti-religious commentators on the Constitution have sometimes argued that the prohibition of religious tests in Article VI proves that religion may not be interjected into American political life. However, these commentators are wrong. The Article states that *"no religious Test shall ever be required as a qualification to any Office or public Trust."* Declining to require a religious test is not the same thing as permitting religious involvement. Every president since George Washington, with the sole exception of Thomas Jefferson, has taken the oath of office with his hand placed on the Bible and ending his oath with the words, *"So help me God,"* which are not part of the prescribed constitutional oath of office. The Constitution's "no religious Test" does not make religious concerns by either the electorate, the candidate, or officers of the government illegitimate.

H.   Article VII: Ratification

Article VII requires only nine states to ratify the Constitution. This provision avoided the almost impossible requirement under the Articles of Confederation for all states to agree upon any action.

I.   The Subscription Clause

> *Done in convention by the unanimous consent of the States present on the seventeenth day of September in the year of our Lord one thousand seven hundred and eighty-seven and of the independence of the United States of America the twelfth. In witness whereof we have hereunto subscribed our names.*

The Subscription Clause is important because it attested to the authenticity of the Constitution as signed by the majority of delegates to the Constitutional Convention. However, this clause is also important because its date connects the Constitution to the God of the Bible and the Christian foundations of America that are identified in the Declaration of Independence, which was issued twelve years earlier. The Subscription Clause declares that America was founded in 1776 with the Declaration of Independence, not upon the signing of the Constitution in 1787.

By embracing 1776 as the birthday of the nation, the Constitution signaled the incorporation of the Declaration of Independence by reference into the Constitution, including all of its foundational theological language and Biblical principles. Rightfully understood, the Subscription Clause ties the Constitution to the Creator God of history. Those who argue to the contrary must specifically ignore the obvious meaning of the Subscription Clause.

This clause is also significant regarding the Christian history of America because our Founders fixed the date of their subscription according to the Gregorian calendar, which had been established during the reign of Pope Gregory XIII (1572-1585), or about two hundred years before the Constitution was written. The Gregorian calendar became known as the Christian calendar because it was anchored to the birth of Jesus. Significantly, from 1606 until 1752, England and her colonies had calculated time based on the Roman calendar, which was not tied to the birth of Jesus. At the time of the Revolution, England had only been using the Gregorian calendar for twenty-four years, yet when the Americans gained independence from England, they did not seek independence from the calendar that designated time from the birth of Christ.

The French Revolution, which occurred only a few years after the American Revolution, included a revolt against the established theological as well as political order. Therefore, the French revolutionaries did not continue to follow the Gregorian calendar, but declared the year of their revolution to be Year One, even eliminating the seven-day theological week in favor of a more secularized ten-day week. The Americans did not revolt against God, but only against England, continuing to use the Gregorian calendar and the seven-day week with Sunday as the day of rest.

III.   THE CALL FOR A BILL OF RIGHTS

The inclusion of a Bill of Rights in the United States Constitution was barely mentioned at the Philadelphia Constitutional Convention in 1787. Most delegates saw it as unnecessary. They believed that the fundamental rights of individuals had been secured by the various individual state constitutions and all power not expressly delegated to the new federal government was reserved to the people.

George Mason, however, did not agree. As one of seven Virginia delegates to the Constitutional Convention, Mason consistently spoke out in favor of the rights of individuals and against centralized governmental authority. Mason, the author of the Virginia Declaration of Rights, was convinced that *"there never was a government over a very extensive country without destroying the liberties of the people."* His attempt at the Convention to include a Bill of Rights in the new Constitution was defeated by a unanimous vote of those present.

Although Mason stood nearly alone at the federal Constitutional Convention, his cry for a Bill of Rights was heeded at the state conventions when they were considering ratification of the Constitution. Mason's refusal to sign the Constitution without a Bill of Rights and his stated objections were published all over the country. Although he did not stop state ratification of the Constitution, he did cause many states to condition their approval on the understanding that a Bill of Rights would be immediately added by the Congress. Mason's own state of Virginia was one of those states.

James Madison was elected as Virginia's delegate to the United States House of Representatives when the first Congress met in New York under the new federal Constitution. Although Madison did not personally see the necessity for a Bill of Rights in the Constitution, he did see the value in proposing such a bill. One of his goals was to pull in the two states—Rhode Island and North Carolina—that had yet to ratify the Constitution. Madison also recognized that a Bill of Rights would satisfy the states that had called for a declaration of rights during the ratification process. Madison expressed his view in these words:

> *[N]otwithstanding the ratification of this system of Government by eleven of the thirteen United States, . . .; yet still there is a great number of our constituents who are dissatisfied with it; among whom are many respectable for their talents and patriotism, and respectable for the jealousy they have for their liberty, which, though mistaken in its object, is laudable in its motive. . . We ought not to disregard their inclination, but, on principles of amity and moderation, conform to their wishes, and expressly declare the great rights of mankind secured under this constitution. The acquiescence which our fellow-citizens show under the Government, calls upon us for a like return of moderation."*

> *I believe that the great mass of the people who opposed it, disliked it because it did not contain effectual provisions against encroachments on particular rights, and those safeguards which they have been long*

accustomed to have interposed between them and the magistrate who exercises the sovereign power; nor ought we to consider them safe, while a great number of our fellow-citizens think these securities necessary.

In discussing the efficacy of a Bill of Rights with James Madison, Thomas Jefferson wrote on March 15, 1789:

The inconveniences of the Declaration are that it may cramp government in its useful exertions. But the evil of this is short-lived, trivial & reparable. The inconveniences of the want of a Declaration are permanent, afflicting & irreparable. They are in constant progression from bad to worse. The executive in our governments is not the sole, it is scarcely the principal object of my jealousy. The tyranny of the legislatures is the most formidable dread at present, and will be for long years. That of the executive will come in it's turn, but it will be at a remote period. . . I am much pleased with the prospect that a declaration of rights will be added.

In June 1789, James Madison introduced a Bill of Rights to the House of Representatives. Although Madison is credited as being the primary author, most of the Bill of Rights, the first ten amendments, were drawn from the proposals made by Mason during the Constitutional Convention two years earlier. The original proposed Bill of

Rights had twelve amendments; however, only ten were actually ratified by the states.

Madison's move in proposing a Bill of Rights to Congress also had the effect of neutralizing New York's call for another constitutional convention. Madison feared that another convention could open Pandora's box and result in the unraveling of the fledgling Constitution. He was successful in thwarting that initiative.

Eventually, Madison was also successful in persuading Congress to approve the proposed Bill of Rights. In doing so, he had to overcome arguments that it was premature to amend a Constitution that was as yet untested and, as a matter of priority, other important business should first be considered.

Nevertheless, Congress submitted a Bill of Rights with twelve amendments to the states for ratification on September 28, 1789. Two of the original twelve were not ratified by the states: one changing the apportionment of Congress and the other forbidding congressional pay raises to take effect until after the next election. (In 1992, this latter proposal became the Twenty-seventh Amendment to the Constitution.)

IV.   THE FEDERALIST PAPERS

After the Constitution was drafted in 1787, it had to be ratified by nine of the thirteen colonies before it could become the law of the land. Because New York was such a pivotal swing state in the approval process for the new Constitution, a series of anonymous, pro-Constitution letters began to appear in the newspapers there under the pseudonym *Publius*. These eighty-five letters to the editor came to be known as *The Federalist Papers* (sometimes called *The Federalist*). They help to shed light on what the Founders intended by the words of the Constitution, since they were written contemporaneously by those who had helped to frame that document.

The Federalist Papers should be required reading for all American law students along with the Declaration of Independence and the Constitution. Most Americans are shocked to discover that these foundational documents are not required reading in most law schools! Therefore, many law students graduate, pass the bar exam, and begin to practice law without having even a vague understanding of the overarching Biblical principles that formed our nation, its Constitution, and its laws.

The real identity of *Publius* was not known in 1789, but we know today that *The Federalist Papers* were written by Alexander Hamilton, James Madison, and John Jay. All three of these writers professed faith in Jesus Christ. Their essays are still sometimes cited in legal briefs and quoted in various court decisions.

In *Federalist No. 15*, Alexander Hamilton, one of the authors, asked and answered the most basic civics question about man's sinful nature:

> *Why has government been instituted at all?*
> *Because the passions of men will not*
> *conform to the dictates of reason and justice*
> *without constraint.*

Federalist No. 55, which is generally attributed to either Hamilton or Madison, discusses the necessity in a republican (or representative) form of government for both the electors and those elected to be of good character:

> *As there is a degree of depravity in mankind which requires a certain degree of circumspection and distrust, so there are other qualities in human nature which justify a certain portion of esteem and confidence. Republican government presupposes the existence of these qualities in a higher degree than any other form.*

Alexander Hamilton pointed out in *Federalist No. 22*:

> *The fabric of American empire ought to rest on the solid basis of THE CONSENT OF THE PEOPLE. The streams of national power ought to flow immediately from that pure, original fountain of all legitimate authority.*

The same thought was emphasized again in *Federalist No. 49*:

> *[T]he people are the only legitimate fountain of power, and it is from them that the constitutional charter, under which the several branches of government hold their power, is derived.*

By placing the authority of government in the consent of the governed, our Founders recognized that ultimately, through the legislature, the majority—"we the people"—were to have the greater say. James Madison points out: "*In republican Government the majority however composed, ultimately give the law.*"

Today, in America, however, we have seen that when secularists do not have a sufficient majority to enact legislation favorable to them, they have taken an alternate route to establish their anti-God agenda through sympathetic judges reinterpreting both our history and the Constitution itself. John Adams, a signer of the Declaration and our nation's second president, argued against such rule by men by affirming the superiority of a republic over a democracy, a nation of laws and not of men. He said:

> *There is no good government, but what is republican. . . . [T]he very definition of a republic is "an empire of laws, and not of men." . . . [T]hat form of government which is best contrived to secure an impartial and exact execution of the laws, is the best of republics.*

Most of the Founders were quite leery of the whole concept of a pure democracy, where the people hold all power directly. Instead, the Founders established this nation as a republic, in which the government functions through elected representatives.

In *Federalist No. 10*, James Madison argued that the elected representatives of the people are able to administer government more wisely than the people themselves acting directly as a pure democracy. He believed that a group of people acting directly would be more easily swayed by their passions toward factionalism than elected representatives who would be more likely to apply their collective wisdom for the best interests of the country as a whole—so long as they were not given to temper, prejudice, or sinister designs.

One of the problems we see today in modern America, where the judiciary has assumed a greater power than originally assigned, is that factionalism has been magnified through court appointments that lead to the political ascendancy of one unelected faction or another. The men who drafted the Constitution viewed the legislative branch as being far more important than the judicial branch. In fact, as the original Founders interpreted the Constitution, the judiciary was expected to be the least important branch of government.

Article I of the Constitution (dealing with the legislature) received much more detailed attention than Article III (dealing with the judiciary). The Founding Fathers never intended for us to live under a "judge-ocracy," where the federal Supreme Court would rule as an oligarchy, remake the laws, and impose the will of the minority on the majority.

Alexander Hamilton pointed out in a footnote in *Federalist No. 78*: "*Of the three powers above mentioned, the judiciary is next to nothing.*" In the same *Federalist*, Hamilton discusses the constitutional dilemma that could arise were the judiciary to assert its will above the will of the people as expressed by the legislature. He concludes that the judiciary is not superior to the legislature, but is primarily "*to keep the latter within the limits assigned to their authority*" and to interpret the laws. However, he concludes that when a conflict develops, it is supposed that "*the power of the people is superior to both.*"

V. THE CONTINUING ROLE OF RELIGION IN ESTABLISHING GOOD GOVERNMENT

Our Founders understood that a constitutional government that placed ultimate power in the hands of the people would ultimately require a virtuous people in order to succeed. Therefore, the Black Regiment, the black-robed preachers who instructed their congregations from the pulpit every Sunday in both theology and politics, were expected to continue to play an important role in instructing the people in virtue.

Seven years before the United States Constitution was written, Massachusetts unveiled its state constitution. One of the influential members of the Black Regiment, Rev. Samuel Cooper of Boston, delivered a sermon in honor of that occasion entitled "A Sermon on the Day of the Commencement of the Constitution." Rev. Cooper discussed the importance of virtue in maintaining good government:

> *[A]s piety and virtue support the honour and happiness of every community, they are peculiarly requisite in a free government. Virtue is the spirit of a republic; for where all power is derived from the people, all depends on their good disposition. If they are impious, factious and selfish; if they are abandoned to idleness, dissipation, luxury, and extravagance; if they are lost to the fear of God, and the love of their country, all is lost. Having got beyond the restraints of a divine authority, they will not brook the control of laws enacted by rulers of their own creating. We may therefore rely that*

the present government will do all it fairly can, by authority and example, to answer the end of its institution, that the members of this commonwealth may lead a quiet and peaceable life in all godliness as well as honesty, and our liberty never be justly reproached as licentiousness.

Coming to the end of this sermon, Rev. Cooper predicted a great future for liberty if both government and citizens pursued a Godly course: *"We seem called by heaven to make a large portion of this globe a seat of knowledge and liberty, of agriculture, commerce, and arts, and what is more important than all, of Christian piety and virtue."*

American Christians need to understand what is at stake today in our nation. Since the 1960s, because of various decisions by the United States Supreme Court favoring secularism over religion, America has begun to stray from its founding Biblical principles. Some Americans seem to want to forget God. We regularly break His laws and no longer think them important to our survival as a nation. Courts have jettisoned major portions of our Judeo-Christian heritage as unconstitutional. We must not forget what John Adams said about virtue being an implied assumption of our constitutional form of government. He warned his countrymen:

[W]e have no government armed with power capable of contending with human passions unbridled by morality and religion. Avarice, ambition, revenge, or gallantry, would break the strongest cords of our Constitution as a whale goes through a net. Our Constitution

*was made only for a moral and religious
people. It is wholly inadequate to the
government of any other.*

VI.   A CAUTIONARY NOTE

As great as the Constitution is, and as much as it
was influenced by the Bible and by the Godly men who
wrote it, we must never put that document on the same
level as the Bible. The Bible should be the only source
upon which Christians base their duties and responsibilities
toward both God and government. The Bible alone is to be
the exclusive source of a Christian's belief about the role of
government—nothing else. A Christian should not base his
religious beliefs upon a source that is less than absolute.
Anything other than the Bible is a flawed source.
Christians should not be drawn astray or misled by people
who use sources other than the Bible to explain a citizen's
responsibility toward government.

Some of the claims made by the Black Regiment
during the Revolutionary War were exaggerated when they
declared that the cause of America was the cause of Christ.
Instead, President Abraham Lincoln struck a better chord
when he pointed out during the Civil War that citizens
should not so much ask whether the Lord is on their side,
but rather, whether they are on the Lord's side.

The United States Constitution should not be used
as a basis for a Christian's religious beliefs. Even though
America's Christian heritage influenced the writing of the
Constitution, there are serious problems with viewing the
Constitution as a source for Christian beliefs because God
did not author it. God authored His Word, and next to His

Word, the Constitution is nothing. No one should raise anything to the status of Scripture! Consider the inferiority of the Constitution when it is compared to the Bible, God's eternal, unchanging Word.

1.   The Constitution is man-conceived.

The initiative to create the Constitution was the idea of men. While some were honorable men, history clearly shows that some were not so honorable. Benjamin Franklin commented upon the men who had gathered for the 1787 Constitutional Convention:

> *[W]hen you assemble a number of men, to have the advantage of their joint wisdom, you inevitably assemble with those men all their prejudices, their passions, their errors of opinion, their local interests, and their selfish views. From such an assembly can a perfect production be expected?*

Clearly, the answer to Franklin's question is that none but God can produce perfection. The United States Constitution is not a perfect document, and Christians should never replace God's Word with the Constitution. To do so will always end in disappointment.

2.   The Constitution is man-written.

Drafting the Constitution was an exercise of compromises among the men assembled at the Constitutional Convention. The writers knew that the colonies would never unite under the Constitution unless everyone gave up some of their demands about such important issues as how to count the slaves and how long the president should be allowed to stay in office. The Constitution is not the document the drafters thought was best; it is the document they thought the colonies would adopt. In contrast, the Word of God does not compromise in any respect; truth cannot be compromised. God wrote His Word with no thought as to whether anyone would accept it. He wrote it because it is truth.

3. The Constitution is man-enforced.

The Constitution is not enforced the same way in every court. Laws are sometimes enforced ten different ways in ten different places. In fact, often there is no absolute standard at all. The standard is whatever the judges think at that time. When men are involved in enforcing law, there will always be sliding standards depending upon who the enforcer may be with any particular issue. But our God is a God of absolutes and always consistently enforces His Word.

4. The Constitution is man-interpreted.

Christians who form any of their religious beliefs upon Constitutional ideas or principles will need to call Washington, D.C. every Monday morning to find out what they believe because every Monday morning Washington leaders have a new way to interpret what the Constitution says. Thankfully, God's Word is not going to change for eternity. The same cannot be said for the Constitution. It only takes five of the nine Supreme Court Justices to change the entire interpretation of the Constitution. Activities that ten years ago were absolutely illegal are now legal. How did that happen? It happened when presidents, with the advice and consent of the Senate, appointed new Supreme Court Justices. So while the Constitution itself remains the same, the men responsible for interpreting it do change, and with their change come different interpretations of the same constitutional phrase. Thus, the Constitution, unlike God's Word, is unstable and should not be the source for a Christian's religious beliefs. As one Supreme Court Justice in the early twentieth century noted: *"[T]he Constitution is what the judges say it is."* In contrast, God's Word is stable. It never changes. But the Constitution is unstable, and judges have placed it in a constant state of flux.

5. The Constitution provides for its own amendment.

Nothing in the Constitution is absolutely sacred. Every bit of it can be changed, even to the people's detriment, if that is what a majority of the people desire. Without a revival and a touch of God on our nation, the Constitution may look very different in a decade or two. On the other hand, even if people try to rewrite the Word of God, it cannot change because God's Word is unchangeable.

While American Christians must take great care to preserve the gifts of freedom and self-government that God has given to us, we must realize that it is God who raises up and tears down nations according to His sovereignty. No Christian should ever equate America with the Kingdom of God.

CHAPTER SIX

THE FIRST AMENDMENT RELIGION CLAUSES IN THE BILL OF RIGHTS

> Some delegates to the Constitutional Convention would not agree to ratify the Constitution without a guarantee that a written Bill of Rights would be speedily enacted to secure religious freedom and other important individual liberties.

When the hard job of getting the states to ratify the new Constitution began, the first problem that surfaced was that many of the states, and even some of the delegates, would not agree to ratify the Constitution without a written Bill of Rights. Patrick Henry, Samuel Adams, and even Thomas Jefferson, who was thousands of miles away in France as our ambassador at the time, were among the many leaders of the founding era who insisted that the Constitution must clearly contain in writing those specific liberties the colonists were intent on preserving.

So, on September 25, 1789, three days after Congress authorized the appointment of paid chaplains, Congress drafted and enacted the first ten amendments to the Constitution, also known as the Bill of Rights, which include the First Amendment with its two important religion clauses: *"Congress shall make no law respecting an establishment of religion, or prohibiting the free exercise thereof."* These two clauses are referred to legally as the Establishment Clause and the Free Exercise Clause. The first is a prohibition, and the second is a guarantee.

I.   THE FIRST AMENDMENT FREEDOMS

Among the most important freedoms we enjoy as Americans are the freedoms of the First Amendment— freedom to associate and to petition the government, freedom of the press, and especially, the freedoms of religion and speech. Our Founding Fathers believed that these rights were paramount to the survival of the new nation. Furthermore, they understood the importance of Christianity to the survival of our nation.

George Washington stated, *"Religion and morality are the essential pillars of civil society."* John Adams recognized, *"Our Constitution was made only for a moral and religious people. It is wholly inadequate to the government of any other."* Finally, Charles Carroll, signer of the Declaration of Independence, remarked, *"Without morals a republic cannot subsist any length of time; they therefore who are decrying the Christian religion whose morality is so sublime and pure . . . are undermining the solid foundation of morals, the best security for the duration of free governments."*

The First Amendment's freedom of religion guarantee is divided by courts into two clauses: the Establishment Clause and the Free Exercise Clause. Each is treated differently by our courts and, therefore, each will be discussed separately.

II. BAPTIST INFLUENCE ON THE FIRST AMENDMENT RELIGION CLAUSES

For two decades prior to the American Revolution, Baptists endured severe religious persecution, particularly in the Anglican colony of Virginia. In Virginia at that time, Baptist pastors were beaten, arrested, and whipped for the offense of being bold for the Gospel as shown by the following examples:

➤ In Fredericksburg, five Baptist preachers were imprisoned in 1768 for a year and a day because they would not promise to stop preaching in the county. While in jail, they continued to preach through the bars.

➤ In Culpeper County, James Ireland preached through his prison bars while horses galloped through the listening crowd and his persecutors urinated in his face. Ireland's enemies failed in their attempts to kill him by gunpowder explosions, suffocation, and poisoning. Instead, many came to Christ through his witness to cellmates sent to harass him during his five months in jail or receipt of letters he wrote *"from my Palace in Culpeper."* Eventually, William and Mary's Toleration Act of 1770 forced his release.

➤ In 1771, the State of Virginia jailed fifty Baptist worshippers for preaching the Gospel contrary to the *Anglican Book of Common Prayer.*

Thomas Jefferson of Virginia stood boldly against such religious oppression. In 1781 he wrote:

> *Millions of innocent men, women, and children, since the introduction of Christianity, have been burnt, tortured, fined, imprisoned; yet we have not advanced one inch towards uniformity. What has been the effect of coercion? To make one half the world fools, and the other half hypocrites. To support roguery and error all over the earth. Let us reflect that it is inhabited by a thousand millions of people. That these profess probably a thousand different systems of religion. That ours is but one of that thousand. That if there be but one right, and ours that one, we should wish to see the 999 wandering sects gathered into the fold of truth. But against such a majority we cannot effect this by force. Reason and persuasion are the only practicable instruments. To make way for these, free enquiry must be indulged; and how can we wish others to indulge it while we refuse it ourselves.*

In 1786, the Virginia legislature adopted Thomas Jefferson's Act for Establishing Religious Freedom. This statute was supported by the Baptist General Association and provided for religious freedom. It said:

> *[N]o man shall be compelled to frequent or support any religious worship, place, or ministry whatsoever, nor shall be enforced, restrained, molested, or [burdened] in his*

*body or goods, nor shall otherwise suffer, on
account of his religious opinions or belief;
but that all men shall be free to profess, and
by argument to maintain, their opinions in
matters of religion, and that the same shall
in no wise diminish, enlarge, or affect their
civil capacities.*

It comes as no surprise, therefore, that Baptists in
Virginia were unwilling to approve the federal Constitution
without a similar guarantee of religious liberty.   John
Leland, the most prominent Virginia Baptist preacher at the
time of the Revolution, took the lead in this struggle for
religious freedom.   An itinerant preacher who traveled
thousands of miles and preached thousands of sermons,
Leland believed religious liberty was an unalienable right
and not a favor granted by any government.   In *The Case
for Religious Liberty*, Leland wrote:

*[W]hen government favors religion, it has
favorites. Some religions will be favored by
the state and some will not. In Virginia, we
Baptists were outsiders. We were not the
favored state church. We had to behave, to
keep a low profile. We had to get a
government license to preach. And worse,
our taxes were used to finance the activities
of the state church. But as for us Baptist
pastors, we would not keep a low profile so
far as the gospel is concerned.*

*The most important thing in my life is to
save souls. The most fertile soil in which
souls can be harvested is the soil of religious
liberty. When men are free to believe or not,*

> *then they can freely respond to the love of
> God. But when the state tries to help
> religion, it inevitably controls religion, and
> it kills the free response of the people, and
> fewer souls are saved.*

James Madison disappointed Virginia Baptists
when he opposed adding a Bill of Rights to the U.S.
Constitution. Madison was satisfied that section 3 of
Article VI provided for religious liberty, namely that: *"No
religious Test shall ever be required as a qualification to
any Office or public trust under the United States."* John
Leland had the opposite opinion as shown in his writings:

> *What is clearest of all—Religious Liberty, is
> not sufficiently secured, No Religious test is
> Required as a qualification to fill any office
> under the United States, but if a Majority of
> Congress with the President favour one
> System more then another, they may oblige
> all others to pay to the support of their
> System as much as they please, and if
> Oppression does not ensue, it will be owing
> to the Mildness of Administration and not to
> any Constitutional defence, and of the
> Manners of People are so far Corrupted,
> that they cannot live by Republican
> principles, it is Very Dangerous leaving
> Religious Liberty at their Mercy.*

As a result, tradition says that Leland was preparing
to oppose Madison as the Orange County candidate to the
1788 Virginia Convention called to ratify the Constitution.
Leland would have been a formidable candidate for
Madison. He was an esteemed leader among the

burgeoning Baptist population of Virginia and had the support of the Virginia Baptist General Committee. After a six-year revival, Baptists had become the most populous sect in the state; and it would have been impossible for Madison to win without their support.

However, Madison and Leland chose to hash out their differences privately instead of at the ballot box. There is good historical evidence to show that Madison and Leland met at Fredericksburg in March of 1788. It is said that in return for Leland withdrawing from the race and throwing Baptist support to Madison, Madison agreed to support a Bill of Rights that would include freedom of religion after the Constitution was adopted.

Madison knew the importance of satisfying Baptist voters in Virginia. He knew that without Baptist support he would not be a delegate at Virginia's ratifying convention; but even worse, Virginia would not ratify the Constitution. He feared the domino effect this could have on other states. Both Madison and Leland were true to their word. Leland encouraged Baptists to support Madison in the election, and Madison introduced the First Amendment as part of the Bill of Rights in Congress on June 7, 1789.

Although Madison's support for the First Amendment was politically motivated, his writings make clear that he stood against the tyranny of religious persecution. He was an ardent supporter of religious liberty. For example, in 1785, he opposed a general tax for the support of teachers of the Christian religion. In his *Memorial and Remonstrance* he wrote these words in opposition to the tax:

1. Because we hold it for a fundamental and undeniable truth, "that religion or the duty which we owe to our Creator and the manner of discharging it, can be directed only by reason and conviction, not by force or violence." The Religion then of every man must be left to the conviction and conscience of every man; and it is the right of every man to exercise it as these may dictate. This right is in its nature an unalienable right. . .

3. . . . Who does not see that the same authority which can establish Christianity, in exclusion of all other Religions, may establish with the same ease any particular sect of Christians, in exclusion of all other Sects? that the same authority which can force a citizen to contribute three pence only of his property for the support of any one establishment, may force him to conform to any other establishment in all cases whatsoever?

4. . . Whilst we assert for ourselves a freedom to embrace, to profess and to observe the Religion which we believe to be of divine origin, we cannot deny an equal freedom to those whose minds have not yet yielded to the evidence which has convinced us. If this freedom be abused, it is an offence against God, not against man: To God, therefore, not to man, must an account of it be rendered. . .

11. . . Torrents of blood have been spilt in the old world by vain attempts of the secular arm to extinguish religious discord by proscribing all difference in religious opinion. Time has at length revealed the true remedy. Every relaxation of narrow and rigorous policy, wherever it has been tried, has been found to assuage the disease. The American Theatre has exhibited proofs that equal and compleat liberty, if it does not wholly eradicate it, sufficiently destroys its malignant influence on the health and prosperity of the State. If with the salutary effects of this system under our own eyes, we begin to contract the bounds of Religious freedom, we know no name that will too severely reproach our folly. . . "

Praise God for the integrity of James Madison and John Leland. Their conviction and strong leadership were crucial elements in the passage of the religion clauses in the First Amendment.

III.   THE ESTABLISHMENT CLAUSE

The Establishment Clause of the First Amendment states that *"Congress shall make no law respecting an establishment of religion . . . ."* The framer's intention was to forbid the federal government from establishing an official state church, such as the Church of England. However, since 1947, this clause has been given a much broader application by courts. Over the last half century, the Establishment Clause has been used by the United States Supreme Court to keep the government from supporting one religion over another as well as to prohibit the government from either directly or indirectly promoting any sort of religious activity.

IV.   THE ESTABLISHMENT CLAUSE AND THE SEPARATION OF CHURCH AND STATE

It should be carefully noted that the First Amendment says absolutely nothing about "the separation of church and state." In fact, that phrase is found nowhere in the Constitution or in the Bill of Rights. "Separation" was a doctrine imposed on America by the United States Supreme Court in a decision, *Everson vs. Board of Education*, interpreting the Establishment Clause in 1947— the middle of the twentieth century, nearly two hundred years after the Clause was drafted. The decision in the *Everson* case, which involved bus transportation to Catholic schools, was written by Justice Hugo Black, a former Klansman who detested Catholics even more than he disliked Negroes or Jews.

This phrase, which is so prevalent in modern court decisions and which is alleged so frequently to represent a legitimate constitutional principle, was first used in 1802 by President Thomas Jefferson in an exchange of letters with the Baptist Association of Danbury, Connecticut, in order to assure the Baptists that the government would never be permitted to interfere with the church. Yet, against all reason, this phrase from a letter written by a man who took no part in the drafting of the First Amendment, has been seized upon by our courts for the past fifty years to deny citizens many of the rights that were once understood to be protected under our Constitution. (See

Appendix 3 for a copy of Jefferson's Letter to the Danbury Baptists.)

The Founders' own understanding of the Establishment Clause does not support the modern view of a complete church-state separation, which is really interpreted by modern courts to mean a separation of God and government. What the Founders themselves meant by "an establishment of religion" in the First Amendment was simply that there should be no officially established national church which citizens would be forced to attend, as there had been in England.

James Madison's original draft of the religion clauses shows his view concerning the "separation of church and state:"

> *The Civil rights of none shall be abridged on account of religious belief or worship, nor shall any national religion be established, nor shall the full and equal rights of conscience be in any manner, or on any pretext, infringed.*

V. JEFFERSON AND THE DANBURY BAPTISTS

In 1801, the Danbury Baptist Association in the state of Connecticut rejoiced at the election of Thomas Jefferson as the third President of the United States. On October 7 they wrote to Jefferson, a fellow believer in religious liberty, saying: *"[We] believe that America's God has raised you up to fill the Chair of State."* The Danbury Baptists complained to Jefferson of religious laws made by Connecticut's government. They feared the Congregationalist Church would become the state-sponsored religion and expressed approval for Jefferson's refusal to *"assume the prerogative of Jehovah and make laws to govern the Kingdom of Christ."* Although the Danbury Baptists understood that Jefferson, as president, could not *"destroy the laws of each State,"* they expressed hope that his sentiment would affect the states *"like the radiant beams of the sun."*

It was Jefferson's response to this letter that is the origin of the infamous phrase "separation of church and state" used in the *Everson* decision. Jefferson's reply on January 1, 1802, showed his agreement with the Danbury Baptists that:

> *Religion is a matter which lies solely between man and his God, that he owes account to none other for his faith or his worship, that the legislative powers of government reach actions only, and not opinions, I contemplate with sovereign reverence that act of the whole American people which declared that their legislature should "make no law respecting an establishment of religion, or prohibiting the free exercise thereof," thus building a wall of separation between Church and State.*

In referring to this "wall of separation" Jefferson was borrowing from the metaphor of Roger Williams, a fellow Baptist and Rhode Island's champion of religious freedom. Williams had previously written of *"a gap in the hedge or wall of separation between the garden of the church and the wilderness of the world."*

Christian scholars interpret Jefferson's Danbury letter in its context. They accept Jefferson's view that religion is a personal matter that should not be regulated by the federal government and that the federal government has no power to change law in the states. They interpret the "wall of separation" in the same way as Roger Williams: as a wall to protect God's garden from the world, to protect the church from the government.

In contrast, non-Christian scholars lift the Danbury letter out of its historical context. They turn the "wall" metaphor on its head and now use it to protect the government from the church, establishing a freedom from religion not known by the Founders. This results in a concerted effort to rid government of any religious influence. Hence, the opposition to Bible reading in schools, official proclamations promoting religious events, nativity scenes in public displays, the posting of the Ten Commandments in and on public buildings, prayer in public places, etc. These secular scholars fail to recognize that the Danbury Baptists would never have rejoiced at Jefferson's election if he stood for removal of religious influence on the government.

In 1947, the Supreme Court gave the "wall" metaphor constitutional standing in *Everson v. Board of Education*. In this case, the Justice Black, writing the Court's majority opinion, said:

> *The First Amendment has erected a wall between church and state. That wall must be kept high and impregnable. We could not approve the slightest breach.*

It is interesting to note that no breach of the wall was actually found in *Everson*. The New Jersey statute permitting the state to reimburse parents for the expense of busing their children to and from private parochial schools was upheld. The Court merely used this decision to introduce a new legal principle which would later be employed in an attempt to completely separate God from government.

In the *Everson* case the Supreme Court also held for the first time that the Establishment Clause of the First Amendment applied to individual states through the Due Process Clause of the Fourteenth Amendment. Prior to this ruling, only the federal government had been constitutionally precluded from establishing a religion. It is this Supreme Court incorporation of the Establishment Clause to state and local governments that now stands in the way of individual states passing legislation that favors religion. Were it not for this application, absent a similar prohibitive state law, local school districts could still permit prayers in public schools.

The *Everson* decision is a clear departure from the views of Thomas Jefferson, the Danbury Baptists, and the Founding Fathers. The First Amendment was not intended to stop the states from establishing a church or from locally favoring a particular religion. Both Jefferson and the Danbury Baptists understood this. Jefferson's reference to the legislature of "the whole American people" demonstrates his understanding that the First Amendment applied to the federal government exclusively. Indeed, on January 23, 1808, Thomas Jefferson wrote to Rev. Samuel Miller:

Certainly no power to prescribe any religious exercise, or to assume authority in religious discipline, has been delegated to the general government. It must then rest with the states, as far as it can be in any human authority. . .

The Danbury Baptists did not even ask Jefferson to apply the First Amendment to the states. They acknowledged, *"The national government cannot destroy the laws of each State,"* rather, they looked to Jefferson's power of persuasion to prevail in Connecticut.

In the ongoing legal odyssey to find the true meaning of the "wall of separation between church and state," it is useful to consider the actions of the Founders after the First Amendment was passed. A review of a sampling of their activities makes it clear that the Founders had no intention of neutralizing government from all religious influence:

> ➤ The House of Representatives called for a national day of prayer and thanksgiving on September 24, 1789—the same day that it passed the First Amendment.

> ➤ From 1789 to today, Congress has authorized chaplains, paid by public funds, to offer prayers in Congress and in the armed services.

> ➤ Jefferson closed the Danbury letter, written in his official capacity as president, with a prayer: *"I reciprocate your kind prayers for the protection and blessing of the common Father and Creator of man."*

➢ On the very day Jefferson sent his letter to the Danbury Baptists he was making plans to attend church services in the House of Representatives.

➢ Jefferson signed a treaty into law in 1803 that provided for a government-funded missionary to the Kaskaskia Indians.

➢ In response to a congressional request on July 9, 1812, President James Madison issued a proclamation recommending a day of public humiliation and prayer to be observed by the people of the United States, with religious solemnity.

➢ In 1832 and 1833, Congress approved land grants to Columbian College (later George Washington University) and Georgetown University, Baptist and Jesuit schools respectively.

➢ The Ten Commandments are inscribed on the wall of the United States Supreme Court.

➢ The Supreme Court begins each session with the prayer: *"God save the United States and this Honorable Court."*

➢ The *New England Primer* was used in public schools despite its many religious references.

➢ Every president has invoked God's name or the equivalent in a prayerful manner in his inaugural address.

The views of our first three presidents on matters of church and state also challenge the viewpoint of our modern courts with regard to a separation of God and government:

> *Of all the dispositions and habits which lead to political prosperity, religion and morality are indispensable supports. . . And let us with caution indulge the supposition that morality can be maintained without religion. . . reason and experience both forbid us to expect that national morality can prevail in exclusion of religious principle. It is substantially true, that virtue or morality is a necessary spring of popular government.*

—George Washington, Farewell Address to the United States, 1796

> *[W]e have no government armed with power capable of contending with human passions unbridled by morality and religion. . . . Our constitution was made only for a moral and religious people. It is wholly inadequate to the government of any other.*

—John Adams, October 11, 1798

> *In matters of religion I have considered that its free exercise is placed by the Constitution independent of the powers of the General Government. I have therefore undertaken on no occasion to prescribe the religious exercises suited to it, but have left them, as the Constitution found them, under the direction and discipline of the church or*

> *state authorities acknowledged by the several religious societies.*
>
> —Thomas Jefferson, *Second Inaugural Address,* March 4, 1805

The intent of the First Amendment and the words and actions of our Founding Fathers, including Thomas Jefferson, clearly demonstrate how the words "the separation of church and state" were originally understood by the Founders. These words were never intended to remove God from government; rather they were intended to keep government from controlling and manipulating religious practices. Unfortunately today, two hundred years after Jefferson wrote the phrase, these words have been turned on those they were intended to protect.

VI. APPLICATION OF THE ESTABLISHMENT CLAUSE UNDER THE FOURTEENTH AMENDMENT

As stated previously, the First Amendment was not originally intended to be applicable to the individual state governments. However, in *Everson v. Board of Education* (1947), the Supreme Court applied the Establishment Clause to the states by means of the judicial "incorporation doctrine," which grew out of the Fourteenth Amendment.

The Court held that neither the state nor the federal government may constitutionally set up a church, nor pass laws that aid one religion, aid all religions, or prefer one religion over another. The Court claimed that Jefferson's high wall of separation between church and state was constitutionally mandated, but this decision, coming nearly two hundred years after the Religion Clauses had been drafted, marked the Court's first discovery of the concept of a constitutionally mandated complete separation between God and government.

The Supreme Court's assault against religion had begun. Over the next half century, the Court continued to use this interpretation of the Establishment Clause to curb religious freedom in public schools. One year later, in *McCollum v. Board of Education* (1948), the Court used the Establishment Clause to strike down voluntary religious classes in public schools, even when parental permission was required before a student could attend.

In the early 1960s, the Supreme Court began using the Establishment Clause to further restrict religious freedom in public schools. In *Engel v. Vitale*, in 1962, the Court invoked the Establishment Clause to strike down prayer in the public schools, even when the prayer was both voluntary and nondenominational.

In 1963, the Supreme Court found voluntary Bible reading in the schools to be unconstitutional in the case of *School District of Abington Township v. Schempp*. In *Epperson v. Arkansas* (1968), the Court struck down a state statute forbidding the teaching of Darwinian evolution. In *Edwards v. Aguillar* (1987), the Court also struck down a state statute mandating that if evolution were taught, creationism must also be taught.

In *Stone v. Graham* (1980), one of its more outrageous decisions, the Supreme Court found a display of the Ten Commandments in the public schools to be unconstitutional. The Court explained:

> *If the posted copies of the Ten Commandments are to have any effect at all, it will be to induce the schoolchildren to read, meditate upon, perhaps to venerate and obey, the Commandments. However desirable this might be as a matter of private devotion, it is not a permissible state objective under the Establishment Clause.*

In 1992, in the case of *Lee v. Weisman*, the Supreme Court struck down clerical invocations and benedictions offered at graduation ceremonies. Some legal analysts see the Court's decision in the *Lee* case as a watershed moment in the Supreme Court's continuing expression of hostility toward religion. In *Lee*, the Court viewed a simple non-sectarian invocation offered by a Rabbi as somehow coercive, dangerous, and harmful to children. Some lower courts have since permitted prayers at graduation if given by students.

In 2000, in the case of *Santa Fe v. Doe*, the Supreme Court determined that prayers offered by students before football games in Texas were unconstitutional because a school policy encouraged the practice and provided a microphone for the students. It appears that a majority of the current Supreme Court Justices have become paranoid about even the simplest official encouragement of religious expression in public schools, despite the fact that the Free Exercise of Religion is the second, and balancing, clause in the First Amendment's Religion Clauses.

VII. IMPLEMENTATION OF THE LEMON TEST TO FIND ESTABLISHMENT CLAUSE VIOLATIONS

The *Lemon* Test was developed by the Supreme Court in a 1971 decision, *Lemon v. Kurtzman*, to determine whether a particular law violated the Establishment Clause. The dispute concerned a Rhode Island law providing a salary supplement to non public school teachers if they agreed not to teach a course in religion. A second law in dispute was a Pennsylvania statute allowing the state to purchase secular educational services from non public schools. The Court used what is now called "The *Lemon* Test" to strike down both laws. Under the *Lemon* Test, a public religious activity will be upheld as constitutional only if it (1) has a predominantly secular purpose; (2) neither inhibits nor advances religion; and (3) creates no excessive entanglement between government and religion.

Some positive decisions have been handed down under the *Lemon* Test in cases involving the Establishment Clause. One notable case was *Lynch v. Donnelly* (1984) where the Court upheld the display of a government-owned nativity scene in Rhode Island, finding that the city had met all three prongs of the *Lemon* test. A few years later in *Westside v. Mergens* (1990), the Court upheld a federal equal access law which stated that schools must allow equal access to school buildings by religious and non-religious groups, as well as by political groups.

In *Lamb's Chapel v. Center Moriches* (1993), the Court overturned a school board decision not to allow the after-school use of school property by a church when it had previously allowed non religious groups to use the property for similar purposes. In *Zobrest v. Catalina Foothills*

(1993), the Court, under *Lemon*, upheld a law that authorized the use of a sign-language interpreter for a deaf student attending a religious school. As recently as 1995, the Court ruled that a university must reimburse publishing costs to a religious student group the same as it reimbursed printing costs for non religious student groups out of the student activity fees. *Rosenberger v. University of Virginia* (1995).

This recent line of Supreme Court decisions is encouraging since the Court has begun to use a test of equal treatment regardless of viewpoint, rather than imposing the strict prongs of the *Lemon* test. The equal treatment and equal access analyses are providing better treatment for religious groups in their use of public facilities such as libraries and in providing equal treatment and equal access for religious groups in schools, colleges and universities. Conservative Justices on the Supreme Court have specifically objected to continuing use of the *Lemon* test in deciding cases based on the Religion Clauses, and this area of law continues to lack clear standards for predicting how the Court might rule in any given case.

VIII. FREEDOM OF RELIGION UNDER THE FREE EXERCISE CLAUSE

In addition to addressing the establishment of religion, the First Amendment also provides that Congress shall not *"prohibit the free exercise"* of religion. Theoretically, this provision means that the government cannot punish or disadvantage a person based upon that person's religious beliefs. While the freedom to believe whatever one desires continues to be absolutely protected, problems sometimes arise when the right to put that belief into action (conduct, as opposed to belief) is limited.

The Free Exercise Clause was made applicable to the states under the "incorporation doctrine" of the Fourteenth Amendment in *Cantwell v. Connecticut* (1940). *Cantwell* involved the conviction of several Jehovah's Witnesses for proselytizing in the streets without a license in such a manner that their hearers were provoked to anger. The Court overturned their convictions but noted that while the freedom to believe is absolute, the freedom to act is not. However, because the statute permitted the licensing official discretion to determine whether the solicitation was for a religious cause, it was unconstitutional.

In the early 1960s, the Court established new standards for determining the validity of state regulations that place incidental burdens on religion. In *Sherbert v. Verner* (1963), the Court set forth a two-part test. First, judges must consider whether there is a substantial burden on the exercise of the person's religion from the law under review. Second, the court must consider whether there is a "compelling state interest" that would outweigh this burden. If the court finds that there is a substantial burden and no compelling state interest, the law will be overturned. On the other hand, if the court finds that there is a compelling state burden, the law may be upheld. The *Sherbert* "compelling state interest" test was the standard of review in free exercise cases until *Wisconsin v. Yoder*.

In the 1972 case of *Wisconsin v. Yoder*, the Court moved away from the "compelling state interest" language used in *Sherbert*, but continued to use a balancing test between the burden on religion and the compelling interest of the government. In *Yoder*, the issue was whether the state could require the children of Amish parents to attend public schools beyond the eighth grade. The Court struck down the law, and in the process set forth the following two-part balancing test: (1) does the law place a burden on the exercise of religion; (2) if so, that burden must then be weighed against the importance of the state interest in the regulation. This legal concept was known as "heightened scrutiny." In short, if the effect of a statute not motivated by an intent to interfere with religiously related conduct nonetheless had an effect on religiously related conduct, the state was required to demonstrate the following:

(1)   That the statute or regulation pursued a particularly important governmental goal; and,

(2)   That an exemption for religious conduct would substantially hinder the fulfillment of that goal.

However, even this balancing test came under negative scrutiny by the Supreme Court in the case of *Employment Division v. Smith* (1990). In *Smith*, the Court articulated yet another new rule for interpreting the Free Exercise Clause. Justice Antonin Scalia, writing the opinion in *Smith*, reversed the previous understanding of Free Exercise analysis by holding that a generally applicable criminal law is automatically enforceable regardless of the degree of burden it causes on an individual's religious beliefs.

At issue in *Smith* was whether the State of Oregon could criminalize possession of the drug peyote and refuse to give an exemption to American Indians whose use of the drug was a central part of their religious rites. The Court held that no balancing of interests test was required so long as the ban on peyote was not motivated by a desire to affect religion. The Court's decision abandoned the principle of "heightened scrutiny" and declared instead that such scrutiny would continue to be applied to a generally applicable statute only when that statute affected both Free Exercise of Religion and some other fundamental constitutional right—what Justice Scalia called a "hybrid situation." Justice Scalia implied that previous cases requiring heightened scrutiny such as *Yoder* were hybrid situations involving Free Speech and Free Exercise. This decision had the negative impact of declaring the Free Exercise Clause to be the only step child in the pantheon of constitutional protections, since it required Free Exercise to be combined with some other recognized constitutional right before it could be given equal protection by the courts.

In *Smith*, the Supreme Court held that there was no violation of Free Exercise because the statute only incidentally and unintentionally burdened religion. Oregon, the Court said, could have legislatively chosen to exempt religious practices from the criminal law, even though it was not constitutionally required to do so.

The dissent in *Smith* argued that strict scrutiny should be applied wherever a generally applicable statute burdens the Free Exercise of Religion. *Smith* was part of an early trend by the Rehnquist Court to curtail Free Exercise rights and enhance the rights of state and local governments.

One important lesson to be learned from the *Smith* decision is that whenever a governmental body enacts general legislation that could have a negative impact on the

Free Exercise of religion, Christian citizens should be alert to insist that the legislature make provision for a religious exemption. Such exemptions for religious exercise will become particularly important as militant gay rights activists continue to press for special recognition under civil rights laws.

In the 1993 case of *Church of the Lukumi Babalu Aye, Inc. v. Hialeah*, the Court found that one Florida city law did unconstitutionally burden religious Free Exercise. In that case, the United States Supreme Court ruled against a Florida city council that had passed a series of "neutrally applicable" ordinances specifically interfering with the practice of animal sacrifice by the Santeria religion. The Court held that, since some non religious exemptions had been included, the government's actions were intended to disfavor a particular religious practice in violation of the Free Exercise Clause.

Alarmed by the Court's suppression of Free Exercise rights, Congress passed the Religious Freedom Restoration Act (RFRA) in 1993 specifically to counteract the bad effect of the *Smith* decision on religious freedom cases. In passing RFRA, Congress recognized that religious freedom could be threatened by generally applicable laws as well as by laws that specifically targeted religion, if religious exemptions were not specifically included. RFRA was an attempt by Congress to reestablish the requirements from *Sherbert* and *Yoder* that government must prove such an overriding interest in burdening religious exercise that the interest could not be met in any way other than the law at issue.

One example of a general law that would be affected by RFRA is one that forbids the wearing of hats in a public building. In enforcing that general law, a conservative Jewish person would also be forbidden to wear a yarmulke in the public building unless the legislation provided a specific exemption for religion. Another example would be a general zoning law prohibiting the establishment of schools in certain sections of a city. Such a law would not specifically target religion because no one, whether religious or not, could have a school in that area. If a church were already established in that section of the city, however, that church could never open a Christian school in its building unless churches were specifically exempted from the law.

Under RFRA, if a generally applicable law substantially burdened the free exercise of religion (such as forbidding a school in an existing church building), the city would be required to have a compelling reason to enforce that law against the church and would need to show that the law was the "least restrictive" way to accomplish the compelling public interest. Many lawsuits were brought and won against governments that passed general laws interfering with religion after the passage of RFRA. Prior to RFRA, these kinds of challenges to general laws did not usually succeed.

However, on June 25, 1997, the United States Supreme Court declared RFRA to be unconstitutional as applied to state law. The Court handed down a decision in the case of *City of Boerne v. Flores* that once again put the status of religious freedom in America in jeopardy. A church in Boerne, Texas, had been prevented from enlarging its building under local zoning laws intended to preserve historical landmarks. The church challenged the law as applied to the church using the principles of RFRA. In the end, however, the United States Supreme Court said the federal RFRA was unconstitutional as applied to state and local governments and held that the preservation law had been appropriately applied to the church.

The Court had two reasons for declaring RFRA to be unconstitutional. First, because RFRA conflicted with the Supreme Court's previous ruling in the *Smith* case, the Court saw RFRA as legislative interference with the judiciary in violation of the constitutional doctrine of separation of powers. Second, the Court said that while Congress may enact laws to protect the free exercise of religion, RFRA could not be enacted under the Fourteenth Amendment as a preventative measure.

While the reasons for finding RFRA unconstitutional as applied to state laws may or may not have been valid, the Court has permitted RFRA to continue to apply to federal laws, such as bankruptcy. Individual states, however, are now required to enact state RFRAs in order to protect the free exercise of religion on a state-by-state basis. Many states have enacted state RFRAs and all states should do so.

The Congress, meanwhile, in another attempt to protect religious expression from the Court, passed the Religious Land Use and Institutionalized Persons Act of 2000 (RLUIPA), which attempts to protect religious expression in the areas of land use and the religious liberties of institutionalized persons. While RLUIPA has also come under constitutional attack in the courts, it has not been declared unconstitutional by the United States Supreme Court.

While these various negative actions by the Court are alarming, some windows for the protection of Free Exercise are still open for twenty-first century Christians.

The free exercise right can be combined with some other constitutional right, such as speech, assembly, or association, and the courts will still protect it.

Individual states may enact their own state RFRA-type legislation, as many have done.

Congress, states, and local governments may enact laws specifically designed to protect freedom of religion in their own jurisdictions, such as the 1998 Religious Liberty and Charitable Donation Protection Act passed by Congress to limit a bankruptcy trustee's power to collect the tithes donated by bankrupt Christians as much as a year before they filed for bankruptcy. Such laws, however, will continue to face constitutional challenges under the Establishment Clause.

Some state courts may reject the federal *Smith* standard and continue to use the *Sherbert/Yoder* analysis to interpret their own state religious freedom clauses.

Citizens can demand that legislatures place religious exemptions in all generally applicable laws that might negatively impact the free exercise of religion. This will be particularly important as militant gay rights activists continue to demand preferential treatment under civil rights laws.

In order for demands for religious exemptions to otherwise generally applicable laws to be successful, Christians must become active participants in the political process at all levels—running for public office on school boards, and local, state and federal legislative bodies, as well as for places on the bench in jurisdictions where judges are elected, or else making sure that candidates for office do not win elections unless they are positively inclined to protect religious liberties.

Despite the fact that it has now become imperative for Christians to pay close attention to the political process in order to protect their Free Exercise rights, we must remember that God is clearly still on the throne. He is never surprised by man's actions. As we are told in Proverbs 21:1: *"The king's heart is in the hand of the LORD, as the rivers of water: he turneth it whithersoever he will."* Nevertheless, God still expects Christians in a democratic political environment to do the work required to protect their religious interests for as long as possible.

CHAPTER SEVEN

FIRST AMENDMENT FREEDOM OF SPEECH AND ITS IMPACT ON RELIGION

Christians have retained more rights under the First Amendment doctrine of Free Speech than under the First Amendment Religion Clauses.

Given the negative court interpretations of the First Amendment Religion Clauses since the mid-twentieth century, Christians have generally been more successful in protecting their Free Exercise rights by using the First Amendment Free Speech Clause. Occasionally, the implied right in the First Amendment to Freedom of Association has also been used to protect the Free Exercise rights of Christians, particularly when groups of Christians are involved.

The Free Speech provisions of the First Amendment have generally been more helpful to Christians in this century than the Free Exercise provisions because of a case decided by the United States Supreme Court in 1878. In the case of *Reynolds v. U.S.*, the Court determined that the right to free exercise of religion related only to beliefs, not to conduct.

The *Reynolds* case involved the right of the government to make bigamy a crime in federal territories. Mormon religious advocates claimed that polygamy was their religious duty and, therefore, should not be criminalized. The United States Supreme Court held that no conduct could be justified when a neutrally applicable law was broken simply because a religious practice commanded it. This was one of the case precedents on which the *Smith* decision was based.

One should remember, however, that the *Reynolds* decision was issued at a time when judges and Justices of the Supreme Court still followed the legal principles of the fixed, uniform, and universal Biblical laws derived from the common law and did not generally decide cases on the basis of evolving precedents. Under that pre-evolutionary common law method, the Court was free in 1878 to determine that polygamy, like human sacrifice, was a religious belief *"in violation of social duties."*

Today, however, in an immoral climate with evolving case precedents, this decision has become a gold mine for precedents that prohibit conduct based on Christian principles. It will be interesting to note how the Supreme Court would handle this prior *Reynolds* decision in the event that same-sex marriage is declared to be a constitutionally protected right. If same-sex couples are granted a constitutional right to marry, how could the Court continue to declare polygamy to be a crime in America?

One problem for Christians in the current legal climate involves the fact that Christianity is more than merely a set of religious beliefs; it is primarily a way of life, a manner of conduct. When the Declaration of Independence was written, the Founders based our liberties, including our religious liberties, on our duties to the Creator God of the Bible. Under the modern legal standards of gradually evolving case precedents, Christians have sometimes been forced to legally cite to the bizarre conduct of offbeat religious groups to protect their Free Exercise rights rather than risk a purist legal argument based on the principles of the Declaration that might actually prohibit their own Christian-based conduct. Such conduct would have been protected as good public policy by a court that still recognized the Biblical basis for American law.

As Christians have been forced to protect more of their conduct (such as the freedom to distribute tracts or to preach on the streets) based on legal principles developed for the Free Speech Clause rather than the Free Exercise Clause, other problems have emerged. Christians, for example, must sometimes argue for the rights of churches to locate in towns based solely on the fact that adult establishments have free speech rights to locate in those same towns.

It is a sad fact of twenty-first century legal jurisprudence that Christians are currently more successful when they defend their religious rights under the Free Speech Clause of the First Amendment than under the Free Exercise Clause. First Amendment Free Speech is one of the most protected rights under the Constitution; but unfortunately, even this right is not absolute when it comes to defending religious liberties.

I. PROTECTION OF SPEECH IN TRADITIONAL PUBLIC FORUMS

Evolving case law, based on the Darwinian model of evolving Court precedents rather than on the fixed, uniform, and universal common law that was in effect when the Constitution was drafted, has determined the parameters of free speech. For instance, in *Hague v. CIO* (1939), the Court held that to regulate speech in traditional public forums (such as streets and parks), the government must use the least restrictive means of achieving legitimate, content neutral objectives. Furthermore, if the government tries to prohibit speech based on the speaker's content or viewpoint alone, the state bears the burden of showing a compelling justification for any infringement on speech. Generally, content and viewpoint controls are disfavored and are struck down by the Court, particularly in traditional public forum areas or in areas the government has designated as being compatible with freedom of speech.

II. TIME, PLACE, AND MANNER RESTRICTIONS ON SPEECH

Time, place, and manner restrictions placed on speech are generally upheld when they are content neutral, provide for adequate communication to the target audience, are the least restrictive means available to accomplish the government's legitimate purpose, and are not vague or overbroad or allow too much discretion on the part of government officials. The government may regulate speech by means of any reasonable time, place, and manner restriction so long as the government leaves a workable alternative for the speaker to get out his message. Because of these requirements, time, place, and manner regulations must be narrowly tailored and may not be substantially broader than necessary to achieve a significant government interest (*Ward v. Rock Against Racism* [1989]).

III.   DISCRETION OF PUBLIC OFFICIALS IN GRANTING LICENSES TO SPEAK

Free speech protections also mandate that public officials not be given overly broad discretion to grant or deny permits or licenses without clearly articulated standards (*Freedman v. Maryland* [1965]). When officials are given the authority to determine who can speak, the courts view such authority, in essence, as content or viewpoint control, and such laws are routinely struck down as unconstitutional (*Forsyth County v. The Nationalist Movement* [1992]; *Lakewood v. Plain Dealer Publishing Co.* [1989]).

IV.   PROTECTIONS GRANTED TO LITERATURE DISTRIBUTION

In the interest of protecting free speech, the Supreme Court has additionally decided that an ordinance may not prohibit all distribution of literature (*Lovell v. Griffin* (1938)). This type of ordinance is unconstitutionally overbroad because it sweeps within its coverage speech and conduct that is protected by the guarantees of the First Amendment. As such, this type of ordinance is a violation of freedom of speech. For purposes of constitutional analysis, written and oral speech receive comparable First Amendment protection. Furthermore, religious speech, including prayer and proselytizing, is generally considered to fall within the speech that the Free Speech clause is intended to protect.

V. TYPES OF SPEECH SUBJECT TO CONSTITUTIONALLY VALID RESTRAINT

Another guarantee under the First Amendment Free Speech clause is that speech may not be prohibited merely because it offends some listeners (*Cantwell v. Connecticut* [1940]). Offense is never a reason to limit freedom of speech. In order for speech to be prohibited, the speech must be legally found to be either obscene, an incitement to violence, or an invitation to fight. Yet offense is often the reason that is illegitimately used to require clearing the square of religious speech.

The legal definition of obscenity requires that speech be patently offensive in such a sexually explicit manner that the average person in the community would find the speech utterly without redeeming social value. Speech becomes an incitement to violence when the speaker's words are likely to trigger imminent violent behavior. Finally, fighting words are not merely offensive language directed to the world at large; instead, they are the speaker's invitation for an immediate brawl.

If speech is merely offensive to some listeners, it does not fall into any of the above-prohibited categories. Any prohibition of speech merely because that speech represents an unpopular viewpoint or offends the hearer cannot be constitutionally upheld.

The First Amendment's guarantees of freedom of religion and speech have continued to preserve the right to witness to others in America. While the Apostles were faced with imprisonment and even execution for spreading the Gospel, thus far the Christian's right to witness has generally continued to be constitutionally protected.

CHAPTER EIGHT

OTHER PROVISIONS OF THE BILL OF RIGHTS

> The Bill of Rights, as enacted, became the first ten amendments to the Constitution.

The first ten amendments to the Constitution enacted by the Congress in 1791, make up the Bill of Rights and were intended to identify important rights the new nation specifically wanted to preserve. The text of the Bill of Rights has remained unchanged for more than two hundred years, although, as with the Articles of the Constitution itself, the interpretation of that text by the courts has changed drastically over time. The following chapter presents an overview of key provisions in the Bill of Rights and a brief commentary on each amendment. (See Appendix 2 for a complete copy of all of the Constitutional Amendments, including the Bill of Rights.)

I.   THE PURPOSE OF THE BILL OF RIGHTS

The first ten amendments to the Constitution are called the Bill of Rights. All were adopted by Congress at the same time, on June 15, 1790. They stand apart as the most basic rights guaranteed under the Constitution.

One fundamental purpose of the Bill of Rights was the preservation of state autonomy. The Founding Fathers thought the Bill of Rights was absolutely necessary for the furtherance of ordered liberty. Without the promise of the Bill of Rights, the Constitution would not have been ratified. Many of the Founders opposed the centralization of power in the federal government without sufficient safeguards for state sovereignty. A group called the "Anti-Federalists" warned at the time that unless specific amendments were added to the Constitution to limit the federal government's power, the federal government might envelop and annul the rights of individual states and citizens.

Because of the Founders' strong opposition to an all-powerful central government, the original purpose of the Bill of Rights was intended to restrict the power of the federal government, not that of the states. Samuel Adams noted that the Bill of Rights was created *"to see a line drawn as clearly as may be between the federal powers vested in Congress and the distinct sovereignty of the several States upon which the private and personal rights of the citizens depend."* This fact was recognized by the United States Supreme Court in the 1833 decision of *Barron v. Baltimore*, in which Chief Justice John Marshall ruled that the Bill of Rights did not apply to the individual state governments.

Following the ratification of the Fourteenth Amendment and the demise of the common law, the Supreme Court began to individually apply the provisions of the Bill of Rights to the states as well as to the federal government through the "incorporation doctrine." The effects of incorporation on First Amendment liberties have been generally positive with respect to free speech protections, while not so positive with respect to the religion clauses.

II.   SPECIFIC PROVISIONS OF THE BILL OF RIGHTS

Most of the provisions of the Bill of Rights have now been incorporated through the Fourteenth Amendment to apply to states as well as to the federal government.

A.   The First Amendment

The crucial amendments under the Bill of Rights start with the First Amendment's protection of religion, speech, press, and the rights of assembly and petition; and the words "separation of church and state" do not appear even once in the First Amendment—or anywhere else in the Constitution.

The First Amendment is often considered the most important amendment in the Bill of Rights. The following excerpt from Virginia's Declaration of Rights (1776) shows how it inspired the First Amendment:

> . . . *all men are equally entitled to the free exercise of religion, according to the dictates of conscience; and that it is the mutual duty of all to practise Christian forbearance, love, and charity toward each other.*

Madison drew the language of the speech clause from amendments suggested by the Pennsylvania state ratifying convention.

Virginia's Declaration also described the freedom of the press as "one of the great bulwarks of liberty." The English Bill of Rights (1689) inspired the right of the people to assemble and petition government.

It is important to remember that constitutional protections apply only with respect to actions of the government. The Constitution does not protect citizens against the actions of private corporations or individuals. The Constitution presumes that the rights of private entities will be protected through contract provisions or specific statutes enacted by legislatures. However, legislatures may not enact any laws that would interfere with constitutionally protected rights as determined today by courts.

It is also important to remember that while persons are granted rights to freedom of speech and press under the First Amendment, the Constitution does not protect such persons from the negative consequences of their exercise of these rights. Libel laws apply even in an atmosphere of free speech and press. Intimidation and harassment are still prohibited.

The First Amendment applies to spoken, written, and symbolic speech, as well as to words, pictures, or symbols. The exercise of one's constitutional rights may not interfere with the exercise of those rights by others. For instance, criminal laws such as those against trespass continue to apply, so the exercise of the right to peaceable assembly does not apply on private property. All constitutional rights must be exercised in such a manner as to not infringe or impair the rights of others. Furthermore, such rights may not be exercised in violation of other duly enacted constitutional laws to protect public and private property and to keep the peace.

The right to petition the government for redress of grievances includes the right to peaceful protest at all levels of government. It also includes the right to circulate petitions and gather signatures to influence the government. All rights protected under the Bill of Rights are subject to adjudication by federal courts.

B.   The Second Amendment

This amendment provides for the *"right of the people to keep and bear Arms."* While seemingly a straightforward provision, this Amendment has generated considerable controversy in modern America, particularly as "gun control" advocates have become politically active. Does the Amendment refer only to state militias, or do ordinary private citizens also have a constitutional right to keep and bear arms as individuals? This controversy is currently playing itself out primarily in the political, rather than the judicial, arena as legislatures consider various laws to restrict and regulate particular types of gun ownership. "Second Amendment" societies have been organized by citizens to oppose gun control laws that would leave citizens defenseless against their government, as well as against others who might seek to cause them harm.

C.   The Third Amendment

This amendment protects the people from soldiers being quartered in their homes *"in time of peace . . . without the consent of the Owner, nor in time of war, but in a manner prescribed by law."* This fundamental protection was an important, direct outgrowth of the quartering of British troops in the American colonies both before and during the War for Independence. The English Petition of Right (1628) also prohibited the king from engaging in this practice.

While it was a great concern to eighteenth century Americans at the time of the Revolution, at the present time its provisions are outmoded and seemingly unnecessary. Nevertheless, at some future time these protections may again become relevant.

D.　　The Fourth Amendment

Under the Fourth Amendment, persons are protected against *"unreasonable searches and seizures"* of their persons and property, including homes and automobiles, as well as briefcases and travel bags—with the exception of "reasonable" searches such as those conducted at airports. Persons are guaranteed that no search warrant will be issued against them without a judicial determination of probable cause.

Virginia's Declaration of Rights was the basis for protection against unreasonable search and seizures. Prior to the Revolutionary War, the British had used Writs of Assistance to search private homes for smuggled goods.

Today, the provisions of both the Fourth and Fifth Amendments apply primarily to criminal proceedings. This amendment has been the source of a great deal of criminal case law and has generally been interpreted to provide broad protections to persons accused of a crime. If police officers violate a person's rights during an investigation, a suspect may be set free without a trial. The amendment may also restrict what evidence can be produced in court during a criminal trial. If evidence was gathered in violation of this amendment, courts have refused to permit it to be admitted as evidence against a defendant.

E. The Fifth Amendment

The Fifth Amendment makes several guarantees to United States citizens, as well as to non citizens: Controversy has developed over its provisions with respect to the Patriot Act, enacted by Congress to propagate domestic aspects of the War on Terror. Which provisions apply only to citizens? How far may the government's arm reach in a time of war? The protections of the Fifth Amendment are personal privileges and must be invoked by the individual in order to be applied to him. Courts, for example, will provide an appropriate and free defense, if necessary, for all defendants.

The rights to a grand jury and against double jeopardy were initiated by James Madison and recognized in New York's Declaration of Rights (1788). The right not to be compelled to give evidence against oneself came from Virginia's Declaration of Rights and was also protected in North Carolina's Declaration of Rights (1789). The right to due process of law was carried forward from the English Bill of Rights.

If a person is convicted of a capital or otherwise infamous crime for which the person may receive greater than a one-year prison sentence, there must be a *"presentment or indictment of a Grand jury, except in cases arising in the land or naval forces, or in the Militia, when in actual service in time of war or public danger."* Crimes involving the armed forces are tried in military courts, where military laws apply.

No person may be tried twice for the same offense—i.e., may not be held in double jeopardy. Nevertheless, a person may be subject to both criminal and civil action for the same offense. As seen in the trial of O.J. Simpson, even when a person is acquitted in criminal court, he may successfully be found liable for the same actions in civil court.

No person may be forced to be a witness against himself—i.e., no self-incrimination. When persons avail themselves of this right, it is called "taking the Fifth Amendment." This amendment has also given rise to the "*Miranda* warnings" made popular by TV crime shows. The name *Miranda* is derived from the case in which the Supreme Court identified this constitutional protection. If this warning is not observed by arresting officers, the defendant may not be legally held.

Fifth Amendment protections assure that no person may be deprived of life, liberty, or property without due process of law. The due process clause provides very broad protections in criminal, civil, and administrative law. Due process generally involves the requirements of notice and a fair hearing. Following passage of an additional due process section in the Fourteenth Amendment, courts have also carved out important areas of "substantive" due process rights which protect certain rights that are considered to be fundamental. These provisions generate broad protections as defined by courts.

Finally, the Fifth Amendment provides that no citizen's private property shall be taken for public use without just compensation. Laws with regard to the taking of property by the government are referred to as laws of "eminent domain." The Supreme Court, however, has been expanding the situations under which public takings are permitted. Initially, such takings were only permitted for public uses such as highways and public buildings. In 2005, however, the Court expanded this permission to include taking private property if the public use is considered to improve economic opportunities for the entire community. The decision was roundly criticized by Congress as well by ordinary property holders worried about their own future.

F.   The Sixth Amendment

This amendment guarantees that, in criminal matters, the accused will be provided with a speedy public trial by an impartial jury; will have full information regarding the accusation; will be permitted to have face-to-face confrontation by the witnesses against him; will participate in a compulsory process for obtaining witnesses; and, will have effective assistance of legal counsel. This right has been incorporated to cover state as well as federal criminal trials.

The right to trial by jury was drawn from the English Magna Carta (1215), Virginia's Declaration of Rights (1776), and North Carolina's Declaration of Rights (1776). Virginia's Declaration also provided the right to be confronted with accusers and witnesses, to call for evidence in his favor, and to a speedy trial. The right to have the assistance of defense counsel was proposed by James Madison and the Pennsylvania delegates from Harrisburg.

It was also protected in North Carolina's Declaration of Rights.

Determinations regarding the implementation of the Fourth, Fifth, and Sixth Amendments have been the subject of numerous court actions in which the rights of persons involved in various criminal actions have been expanded on a case-by-case basis. Expansions of the rights guaranteed by these amendments were especially common during the years of the Warren Court in the 1950s and 60s, denoting the time that former governor of California, Earl Warren, served as Chief Justice of the United States Supreme Court.

G.   The Seventh Amendment

The Seventh Amendment provides the basis for determining when jury trials are constitutionally required. The reference to the common law in this amendment no longer applies to the common law that existed at the time of America's founding, but now merely distinguishes matters involving trial by jury as opposed to matters in equity where no law exists or matters considered under admiralty, maritime, or patent law. Courts have provided for specific requirements to be followed in jury selection and procedure. While a suit under patent law is not triable by a jury, a lawsuit regarding infringement of a patent with a demand for an accounting and money damages may be tried by a jury.

H.   The Eighth Amendment

This amendment provides a guarantee against "excessive bail" and "excessive fines" being imposed. It also protects against "cruel and unusual punishment" being inflicted.

The English Bill of Rights and Virginia's Declaration of Rights inspired the prohibition on excessive bail and fines and cruel and unusual punishment.

The key controversies that impact modern interpretations of this amendment generally involve the limits of what punishment is considered "cruel and unusual." Some opponents of the death penalty have argued that in modern America, the death penalty itself constitutes cruel and unusual punishment even though that inclusion was clearly not part of the original intent of this amendment.

I.   The Ninth Amendment

The Ninth Amendment was written to protect those common law rights belonging to the people but not specifically named in the Constitution against an invasion by the federal government. Today, such rights are very limited indeed, although this amendment has been one of the amendments used by courts to find an implied right to privacy in the Constitution, such as the right to privacy involved in cases of contraception, abortion, or gay rights.

J.   The Tenth Amendment

Our Constitution provides for a government of delegated and specifically enumerated powers. The Tenth Amendment was intended to preserve those powers not specifically given by the states to the federal government. The issue of "federalism," or which rights are reserved for the states and the people, is an ongoing concern of federal courts and constitutes a somewhat moving target from court to court and from issue to issue.

James Madison admitted that these words might be deemed unnecessary because the Constitution, as written, intended the same. However, he proposed this amendment because it did no harm and appeased the states who wanted this principle specifically articulated.

This amendment expresses the fact that the federal government may not claim powers that are not granted to it by the Constitution. As we have seen, however, historically there have been very few circumstances in which courts have not found some constitutional provision or other on which to base a federal jurisdiction when the court desires to find one.

III.   THE BILL OF RIGHTS AS APPLIED TO THE STATES BY THE FOURTEENTH AMENDMENT

The Bill of Rights was written to protect the people from the federal government, and was not originally applicable to the states. This fact was recognized in 1833 by the Supreme Court prior to the Civil War (*Barron v. Mayor and City Council of Baltimore*).

Prior to the 1930s, the Supreme Court refused to find the Bill of Rights applicable to the states under the Fourteenth Amendment. The Fourteenth Amendment was ratified with the intention of ensuring that former slaves were given all the privileges and rights conveyed by being a citizen either of the state or the nation. However, today, almost all the rights contained in the Bill of Rights have been made applicable to the states through the Fourteenth Amendment, including all of the rights in the First Amendment, Fourth Amendment, Fifth Amendment, Sixth Amendment (due process clause), and Eighth Amendment.

Beginning in 1937, the powers of the federal government were expanded when the Supreme Court took an entirely different approach to the meaning of the Commerce Clause contained in Article I. One of the key effects of these Commerce Clause cases was the denial by the Court that the Tenth Amendment imposed a general limit upon the subjects of federal power. This change in the Court's view of the Commerce Clause has greatly affected three areas: civil rights legislation, federal criminal laws concerning crimes that were traditionally considered to be local crimes, and the regulation of activities of state governmental entities.

A.   Civil Rights Legislation

In 1964, the Supreme Court upheld the constitutionality of Title II of the Civil Rights Act. The law imposed penalties on anyone who deprived another person of the equal enjoyment of places of public accommodation on the basis of race, color, religion, or national origin. The Court rejected implied Tenth Amendment prohibitions and broadened the meaning of the Commerce Clause in order to legitimate its decision.

> ➢ In *Heart of Atlanta Motel, Inc. v. United States* (1964), the Court held that commerce power legislation would be upheld if there were any arguable connections between the regulation

and commerce which touched more than one state.

➤ In *Katzenbach v. McClung* (1964), the Supreme Court held that Title II was applicable to Ollie's Barbecue, a family-owned restaurant in Birmingham, Alabama, which was more than a mile away from an interstate highway. The Court said that since Ollie's had purchased meat from a supplier who had received it from out of state, that purchase brought the restaurant under the act and sustained commerce power over it.

B.   Federal Criminal Laws

Under the Commerce Clause, Congress may declare as criminal an activity which either relates to interstate transactions, has an effect on interstate commerce, or is necessary and proper to regulate or to effectuate the commerce power. Among the more famous laws passed under this provision are:

➤ The Mann Act, which outlaws the transportation of women for immoral purposes.

➤ The Dyer Act, which punishes the interstate transportation of stolen vehicles.

➤ The Lindbergh Law, which punishes kidnappings that are related to interstate transportation or commerce.

C.   Regulation of State and Local Government Entities

Since 1985, the Supreme Court has refused to recognize that either the Tenth Amendment or the structure of the federal system restricts Congress's power to apply otherwise valid commercial regulations to state or local governments.   This was a reversal of prior case law, although further expansion of Commerce Clause power has slowed in recent years.

CHAPTER NINE

OTHER CONSTITUTIONAL AMENDMENTS

> In the more than two hundred years since the Constitution and Bill of Rights were adopted, only seventeen amendments have been ratified.

Only seventeen amendments to the Constitution have been enacted by Congress and ratified by the states since the Bill of Rights was enacted in 1791. Only one of those amendments was later repealed. The following commentary presents an overview of key provisions from the remaining amendments. (See Appendix 2 for a complete copy of the Amendments to the Constitution, which includes the Bill of Rights and the other Amendments.)

I.   THE INITIAL POST BILL OF RIGHTS AMENDMENTS

Although the Constitution provides for the proposal of amendments by a Constitutional Convention called by the states, to date all of the proposed amendments have been enacted by the Congress.

A.   The Eleventh Amendment

The Eleventh Amendment was proposed by the Third Congress and ratified by the states in 1798.   This amendment provides for governmental immunity from lawsuits by *"Citizens of another State, or by Citizens or Subjects of any Foreign State."* Lawsuits may, however, be brought against an officer of a state if the acts alleged fall out of the scope of that official's constitutional duties. Much litigation in recent years has been focused on determining the parameters of when lawsuits may be brought against individual government officials and when the government itself is protected by sovereign immunity.

B.   The Twelfth Amendment

The Twelfth Amendment, ratified in 1804, provides specific procedures for the Electoral College in voting for the offices of president and vice president.

II.   THE POST CIVIL WAR AMENDMENTS

Following ratification of the Twelfth Amendment, there would be more than a half-century and an intervening Civil War before the Constitution was amended again.

A.   The Thirteenth Amendment (1865)

Following the Civil War, the Thirteenth Amendment abolished slavery and involuntary servitude. Courts have held that neither hard labor as part of a criminal sentence nor conscription into the military fall under the proscriptions of this amendment.

The Thirteenth Amendment is the only amendment that limits both individual and governmental actions: therefore, individuals may not own slaves and governments may not support slavery.

B.   The Fourteenth Amendment (1868)

The Fourteenth Amendment granted certain protections to citizens against the power of the state. The provisions of this amendment are far reaching, and have been the means used to apply many of the first ten amendments to the states through the "incorporation doctrine."

First, the Fourteenth Amendment stipulates that no state can abridge the privileges and immunities of citizens of the United States. This means that residents of one state are entitled to receive the same treatment as non residents or members of other states. Generally, no preferential treatment can be given to in-state residents. An exception arises when a state resident is participating in an activity that bears on the vitality of the nation as a whole, and the state has a substantial reason for giving its own residents preference.

Additionally, the Fourteenth Amendment decrees that no state may deprive any person of life, liberty, or property without due process of law. Due process is comprised of two elements: notice and an opportunity to be heard. Unless a citizen receives warning that his behavior is in violation of the law, and additionally, has a chance to be heard in front of an impartial decision maker, he has been deprived of due process under the Fourteenth Amendment. Due process, as we have seen with the Fifth Amendment involves both procedural due process and substantive due process (which is the protection of rights that are considered fundamental).

The Equal Protection clause of the Fourteenth Amendment prohibits any state from depriving any person in its jurisdiction of the equal protection of law. Specifically, if a law discriminates against a person because of race/ethnic origin, alienage/citizenship, gender, illegitimacy, or if the state's law impedes the exercise of a citizen's fundamental right, the state's law is subjected to a more rigorous standard of scrutiny. The burden rests on the state to show that a particular state interest warrants discriminatory treatment of its citizens. This section of the amendment simply means that the law guarantees equal treatment under the same conditions and among persons who are similarly situated. Today, the Fourteenth Amendment is often used to require the government to treat its religious citizens in the same way that it treats its secular citizens.

The Fourteenth Amendment also disqualifies a person from holding any political or military office if that person has been guilty of rebellion or treason, although Congress may by a two-thirds vote remove the disability from an individual. Finally, this amendment justifies the validity of any public debt of the United States.

C.   The Fifteenth Amendment (1870)

This amendment guarantees the right of every U.S. citizen to vote regardless of *"race, color, or previous condition of servitude."* The provision was considered necessary after freeing the slaves in order to guarantee their voting rights as free citizens. Congress passed the first voting rights act (originally called The Enforcement Act) under this amendment in 1870. The act was broadened after the Civil Rights Movement in 1964 and again in 1965, when it was first referred to as the Voting Rights Act.

III.   KEY AMENDMENTS OF THE TWENTIETH CENTURY

A.   The Sixteenth Amendment (1913)

The Sixteenth Amendment gave Congress the power to collect graduated taxes based on income. This repealed Article I, §9, cl. 4 of the Constitution that prohibited direct federal taxation of a state's citizens that was disproportionate to the number of the state's seats in Congress.

B.   The Seventeenth Amendment (1913)

This amendment, also ratified in 1913, changed the manner in which senators were elected. Under the original Constitution, senators were selected by their state legislators. This amendment provided for the direct election of senators by the people of each state. A state's executive officer may make temporary appointments in the event of a vacancy in the office until an election is held. One commentator notes that since this amendment the national government has grown at the expense of the states.

C.   The Eighteenth Amendment (1919)

This amendment was repealed by the Twenty-first Amendment in 1933. Popularly known as Prohibition, it was a failed attempt to outlaw the sale of liquor in the United States. This is the only constitutional amendment to have later been repealed.

D.   The Nineteenth Amendment (1920)

This amendment gave women the right to vote, popularly referred to as "women's suffrage." All American women were granted the right to vote after decades of agitation and protest. The amendment had first been introduced in Congress in 1878.

E.   The Twentieth Amendment (1933)

This amendment sets the precise date for the ending of one presidential term of office and the start of the following term. The date is fixed at noon on the third day of January in the year in which such terms would have ended. Transportation had reached a point of reliability where such a date could be fixed by law following an election. This amendment also provided for the manner of selecting the person who is to act as president when neither the president or vice president is qualified or available.

Congress has provided by code for a detailed order of succession to the office of President.

F.   The Twenty-First Amendment (1933)

This amendment repealed the Eighteenth Amendment and Prohibition. It also provides for states and localities to continue to enact laws either prohibiting or regulating the sale of liquor within their own borders.

G.   The Twenty-Second Amendment (1951)

This amendment specified that no person should serve as president more than twice. President George Washington had hoped to set a precedent during his time in office by serving only two terms; however, President Franklin D. Roosevelt served four terms and died in office. It is considered the anti-FDR amendment because it passed Congress on March 24, 1947, during Franklin Roosevelt's fourth term as President.

It is designed to prevent the rise of future would-be Caesars. The amendment achieved President Washington's original goal of limiting the lust for power by permitting a president to serve for only two terms.

H.   The Twenty-Third Amendment (1961)

This amendment provides for the District of Columbia, the seat of government, to participate in the Electoral College for the election of president and vice president. The number of electors would be equal to the number of representatives to the House of Representatives and to the Senate, acting in the same manner as those of a state, except that the number of such electors may never exceed that of the least populous state.

I. The Twenty-Fourth Amendment (1964)

This amendment prohibited the use of poll taxes to prevent citizens from voting. It followed on the heels of the civil rights movement that gained voting rights for minorities in a previously segregated South.

J. The Twenty-Fifth Amendment (1967)

This amendment adds to the succession of the vice president to the presidency under the terms of the Constitution and provides for the new president to appoint a new vice president, with the confirmation of two-thirds of the Senate. It also provides a procedure in the event of the temporary disability of the president. The vice president and the cabinet may determine such disability, either physical or emotional, at which point the vice president becomes the acting president until the president informs the leaders of the House and Senate that the disability no longer exists and he resumes his office. This provision may be used in a very temporary manner, such as when the president undergoes anesthesia during surgery, in order to provide for a continuity of the office.

K. The Twenty-Sixth Amendment (1971)

The Twenty-sixth Amendment lowered the voting age from twenty-one to eighteen, the age at which citizens at that time could be conscripted for military service.

L.   The Twenty-Seventh Amendment (1992)

This amendment does not permit a variation in the compensation of senators and representatives unless an election of representatives has intervened.   While this amendment had been included in the original Bill of Rights, it was not ratified at that time.

IV.   SOME AMENDMENTS NOT RATIFIED.

To date, while only twenty-seven amendments have been proposed by Congress and ratified by the states, thousands of other amendments have failed. For example, after the Civil War when the common law was coming under attack by modern jurists looking to remove the law from its foundation in the Bible and evolve it in ways that could be used to manipulate the general society, there were several unsuccessful attempts to provide for the acknowledgement of God and the authority of His law in the Preamble of the Constitution.

A.   The Blaine Amendment

The religion controversy was reflected in the national Congress in 1875 when President Ulysses S. Grant responded to mounting anti-Catholic political pressure by publicly vowing to *"encourage free schools, and resolve that not one dollar be appropriated to support any sectarian [meaning, Catholic] schools."*   To implement this vow, the Speaker of the House of Representatives, James G. Blaine of Maine who was courting the anti-Catholic vote in his bid for the Presidential nomination of the Republican Party, introduced a bill into the Congress that was intended to become the Sixteenth Amendment to the U.S. Constitution.

Blaine's Amendment, as proposed, read as follows:

No state shall make any law respecting an establishment of religion, or prohibiting the free exercise thereof; and no money raised by taxation in any State for the support of public schools, or derived from any public fund therefore, nor any public lands devoted thereto, shall ever be under the control of any religious sect [read, Catholic religious sect]; nor shall any money so raised or lands so devoted be divided between religious sects and denominations.

Blaine's Amendment failed to gain the required two-thirds majority in the Senate by four votes. Nevertheless, federal control over education became more prevalent after the Civil War and in the establishment of the western territories as Americans hoped to use education to attain more uniformity of philosophy among citizens. States were encouraged to put Blaine-like provisions into their state constitutions in order to encourage Catholics to attend public schools. As these anti-Catholic sentiments were enacted into law, the public, or common, school system continued to develop as a Protestant bailiwick, while Catholics developed their own private school system without public money.

This basis of these religious controversies was not lost on anti-Christian humanists, such as John Dewey, who by the 1920s were seeking ways to remove religion entirely from the public school arena. These humanists began to reinterpret Blaine-like provisions in state law against "sectarian" schools. Instead of interpreting "sectarian" to mean "Catholic," the humanists began a campaign to interpret "sectarian" to incorporate Protestant religions as well. Their goal was to remove religion entirely from the public schools.

By the 1960s, humanists had taken control of both the educational establishment and the courts, both being necessary to accomplish their goal. The Blaine Amendment's "sectarian" language has become the battle cry of humanists opposed to all religion in public schools. In the 1960s, both prayer and Bible reading, whether from the Catholic or Protestant Bible, were removed from the public schools as "sectarian" exercises that violated the new constitutional principle of "separation of church and state."

B.   The Equal Rights Amendment

One of the most famous amendments to fail after decades of attempting to have it ratified by the states was the Equal Rights Amendment (ERA). The Equal Rights Amendment was intended to guarantee the absolute equality of men and women under the law. It stated: *"Equality of rights under the law shall not be denied or abridged by the United States or by any state on account of sex."*

The ERA was written in 1923 by Alice Paul, a suffragist leader and founder of the National Woman's Party. She and the NWP considered the ERA to be the next necessary step after the Nineteenth Amendment (woman's suffrage) in guaranteeing "equal justice under law" to all citizens. The ERA was introduced into every session of

Congress between 1923 and 1972, when it was finally passed and sent to the states for ratification.

Generally, states have seven years to ratify an amendment. In this case, conservative women, led by activist Phyllis Schalafly, who were opposed to the amendment because of its potential unintended negative consequences for women and for society in general, organized to defeat its passage in state legislatures. By the time the seven-year time limit had ended, only thirty-five states had ratified the amendment, three short of the thirty-eight necessary for ratification. Congress then extended the seven-year deadline for states to ratify the amendment to June 30, 1982, but even by that deadline, no other states were added to the total needed. Since that time, the amendment has been reintroduced into every session of Congress but has consistently failed to pass. The good that this amendment was intended to do for women has now been achieved through other methods, and the negative consequences have been avoided. Only radical feminists continue to support passage of the amendment.

C.   The 108th Congress

Fifty bills proposing amendments to the Constitution of the United States were introduced into the 108th Congress (2003) alone. Many of these proposed amendments were attempts to check the extraordinary powers being exercised by the federal judiciary contrary to the will of the people. The following proposed constitutional amendments introduced in the 108th Congress specifically focused on moral and religious issues; however, all failed to pass:

To declare that it is not an establishment of religion for teachers in a public school to recite, or to lead willing students in the recitation of the Pledge of Allegiance.

About two million Americans have signed an Internet pledge in support of this amendment. The following statement was a direct response to the Ninth Circuit Court of Appeals decision finding the recitation of the Pledge of Allegiance in public schools unconstitutional, a decision that was dismissed by the United States Supreme Court in 2004 without determining the substantive issue involved:

People retain the right to pray and to recognize their religious beliefs, heritage, and traditions on public property, including schools.

This School Prayer Amendment would override the U.S. Supreme Court's 1962 decision that banned government-sponsored prayer in classrooms. It is also intended to protect the Pledge of Allegiance to the Flag and the display of the Ten Commandments.

V.   THE PROPOSED FEDERAL MARRIAGE AMENDMENT (FMA)

In 2004, the Senate narrowly defeated a proposed amendment that would define marriage as solely between one man and one woman. The proposed amendment states:

Marriage in the United States shall consist only of the union of a man and a woman. Neither this Constitution nor the constitution

*of any state, shall be construed to require
that marriage or the legal incidents thereof
be conferred upon any union other than the
union of a man and a woman.*

The FMA was introduced in the House and the
Senate by pro-family leaders in order to nullify decisions
such as the *Goodridge* decision by the Massachusetts state
supreme court, which now grants marital status to
homosexuals in that state. With activist courts now
involved in the process, the ratification of a constitutional
amendment is probably the only way to guarantee the
preservation of traditional male/female marriage in
America. Because of the likely effects of the Full Faith and
Credit Clause of the U.S. Constitution, discussed
previously, state statutes aiming to preserve marriage (such
as state Defense of Marriage Acts—DOMAs) have not and
will not pose a significant barrier to the homosexual
agenda. Nevertheless, DOMAs have been enacted by
thirty-eight state legislatures signaling that a Federal
Marriage Amendment would likely gain the 38 states
needed for ratification if it can achieve passage in the
House and Senate. In addition, nineteen states have
proposed amendments to their state constitutions limiting
marriage to one man and one woman.

Ratification of the FMA will not automatically
guarantee that homosexual couples would be prevented
from gaining legal status of some sort, short of marriage.
Some pro-family groups have criticized the FMA because it
leaves the door open for states to create civil unions for
same-sex couples. These groups argue that the FMA would
preserve only the meaning of the word "marriage," but
would not protect the practical benefits of the legal
institution itself. Civil unions could achieve all the benefits

and protections of traditional marriages by merely calling the same-sex union by another name.

Liberal opponents of the FMA argue that it would be the first Constitutional amendment to "restrict" the scope of potential individual rights in America rather than expanding such rights. Even some pro-family opponents of the FMA argue that, while it would be a good thing to constitutionally limit marriage to its traditional understanding, the FMA could set a dangerous precedent for the future if the political landscape were to shift decidedly to the left. Could other rights, particularly rights of religious people, then also be constitutionally restricted rather than expanded?

Despite these dangers, most pro-family groups believe that the preservation of traditional, God-ordained marriage, as it has existed for all of human history, is important enough to take the risk of potential negative consequences in the future. They argue that the FMA should be enacted and other potential future consequences should be addressed on their own merits when and if they arise. While the first vote on the FMA was defeated in the Senate in 2004, more votes will follow.

A constitutional amendment requires approval by two-thirds of the House of Representatives and Senate, as well as ratification by three-fourths of the states. The task of gaining approval for a constitutional amendment is overwhelming, but the consequence of doing nothing with respect to preserving the God-ordained family is unthinkable. A society that permits the judiciary to elevate individual rights above public morality is doomed. Christians, in such circumstances, have a moral duty to defend the Constitution through use of the constitutional amendment process.

CHAPTER TEN

THE MODERN COURT'S INTERPRETATION OF THE CONSTITUTION

Methods of judicial review and the adoption of an evolving case method of law to replace the common law have been the primary methods used by judges to expand the constitution.

As Attorney David C. Gibbs III was attending one of his first classes as a first-year law student at Duke Law School, the professor began to introduce himself. He had clerked for the highest levels of our federal courts, including serving as clerk for two different Supreme Court Justices. He had an impressive career in the private practice of law, but had dedicated himself, while still a young man, to teaching future lawyers as a law professor at Duke. This was his opening lecture, one that was more philosophical in nature, but one that he deemed to be the most important.

As the professor began the class, he stated that what he was about to tell the students was the most important change in the law that had happened during his lifetime and while the students would not recognize it now, this change would greatly impact the legal careers of every future lawyer.

He told the class that while they might not fully understand what he was about to say, they should be sure to write it down because it was very important. All the students prepared to write. This was certainly going to be on a test at some point!

The professor declared that the biggest change to have occurred in American law was the fact that the common law is now dead in America.

At that time, the class had no idea what he was talking about. The only common law most of them had ever heard about was "common law marriage" where people could become married in the eyes of the law if they had lived together out of wedlock for a long enough period of time. The students imagined that since so many people were now living together out of wedlock that meant these legally imposed marriages were no longer necessary. The professor interrupted these thoughts and continued:

> *We now live in the era of statutory law. That is the largest change in jurisprudence since America was founded as a nation. It has happened in my lifetime, and while you may not fully understand what I am saying— remember this—it will impact your lives, your families, and your future practice of law. The common law is dead. We now live in the era of statutory law.*

It wasn't until a few years into the law school process that the students began to see the full import of what their professor had said. The common law was a Bible-based law that the American colonies had adopted from England. It provided an absolute standard to under gird the law. The Word of God was the basis for what was right and wrong under the common law.

By telling the class that common law is now dead in America, the professor was letting the students know that any absolute standard in the law has now been replaced. The Bible is no longer the standard for American law. Historical case precedents from years ago are no longer controlling in this new era.

By recognizing that Americans now live in the new era of statutory law, the professor was letting his class know that the law is no longer something " fixed, uniform, and universal" at all times and in all places, as the Founders had believed. Statutory law is now basically what 51% of those voting agree on in any given legislative body. It is a man-made law based on what 51% think is best at any moment. In Biblical terms, we could say that statutory law is essentially men *"doing what is right in their own eyes."*

Years ago, men would do what they thought to be best in light of the common law —the standard of the Word of God. Now this Duke Law School professor must let every class of law students in on the secret—that America no longer has any definite standards for the law. Whatever men think to be best now takes on fancy terms like "meeting societal needs" and "determining good public policy," but the truth is clear. The Bible no longer sets the standard for American law. Legislators and judges now write the laws, determine the policies, and decide the cases based on what they think is best for America—their own personal preferences.

The professor's declaration has taken on an even more dramatic impact as lawyers for the Christian Law Association watch the law unfold during their legal careers. A whole generation of adults has now gone to public schools where prayer and Bible reading were not allowed. A whole generation of adults has watched abortion now consume the lives of approximately fifty million unborn babies. A whole generation of adults has watched homosexuality come out of the closet, become non-criminal, move into being a fashionable special interest group, and now finally becoming a constitutionally protected category demanding all the rights and privileges of marriage, adoption, and other legal benefits and privileges traditionally only given to married people. This generation now sits in the courts, on juries, and in the legislatures making decisions based on what they think is best, but they have little or no connection with America's heritage.

America was founded as a nation by religious men who understood Biblical truth and principles. These principles motivated and controlled their decisions. The America they founded is now having its future shaped and its past re-characterized by judges who are unfamiliar with the Bible, who are uncomfortable with organized religion, and who are unwilling to be controlled by any dominant authority or principle. Their thoughts, feelings, and emotions on any given issue control their decisions because there is no absolute Truth they feel obligated to respect as a controlling authority in their lives.

I. JUDICIAL REVIEW

The concept of "judicial review" has shaped American jurisprudence like no other. The term itself is not found in the Constitution. Section 2 of Article III lists the enumerated powers of the court.

> *Section 2. The judicial Power shall extend to all Cases, in Law and Equity, arising under this Constitution, the Laws of the United States, and Treaties made, or which shall be made, under their Authority; - to all Cases affecting Ambassadors, other public Ministers and Counsels; - to all cases of admiralty and maritime Jurisdiction; - to Controversies to which the United States shall be a Party; - to Controversies between two or more States; - between a State and Citizens of another State; - between Citizens of different States, - between Citizens of the same State claiming Lands under Grants of different States, and between a State, or the Citizens thereof, and foreign States, Citizens or Subjects.*

In spite of its noticeable absence in the Constitution, the judicial review doctrine has been used to some extent by judges almost from the beginning. It is under the doctrine of judicial review that the Supreme Court has given constitutional protection to freedoms and rights that were not specifically enumerated therein. In short, judicial review has permitted the Justices of the Supreme Court to impose their own biases, prejudices, and desires on the rest of the nation under the guise of constitutional interpretation.

The Supreme Court first asserted its right to judicial review of all actions taken by the other branches of government in the case of *Marbury v. Madison* (1803). This is the most famous decision handed down by the Marshall Court; and it was important for at least two reasons. First, the Court marked new territory by claiming a judicial power to review the acts of other branches of the federal government. Additionally, this case signified the first time the Supreme Court declared an act of Congress to be unconstitutional. This would only happen one other time before the Civil War.

Even though today few would argue that the Court does not have the power of judicial review, such was not the case when Chief Justice John Marshall authored the *Marbury* decision. However, after this landmark decision, the assertion that the Supreme Court had the authority to interpret the Constitution and to void the acts of other branches of government on this basis was rapidly accepted. This decision established the Supreme Court as the supreme keeper of the Constitution to the exclusion of the executive and legislative branches of our government.

In a series of cases from 1803, when *Marbury* was decided, until 1821, the Court granted to itself...

> ➤ Power to review the acts of other branches of the federal government, and the authority to declare such acts unconstitutional (*Marbury v. Madison* [1803]);

> ➤ Power to invalidate a state law under the Constitution (*Fletcher v. Peck*]1810]);

➢ Authority to be the single, final interpreter of federal law and the Constitution (*Martin v. Hunter's Lessee* [1816]); and

➢ Authority to review state criminal proceedings (*Cohens v. Virginia* [1821]).

Thus, the stage was set for a radical future expansion of the Constitution by the judiciary.

II.   PHILOSOPHICAL EXPANSION OF THE CONSTITUTION

Three philosophical methods have been used by judges to interpret the U. S. Constitution:

1.   **Strict construction**, which interprets the document to mean exactly what it states and nothing more or less

2.   **Historical approach**, which interprets the Constitution by analyzing its history and what was meant at the time of its writing

3.   **Liberal approach**, which views the Constitution as a "living document" in the sense that its words and phrases must be interpreted in light of our modern desires and the needs of our modern society and not according to the intent of its authors

Today, a majority of lower court judges and Supreme Court Justices use the liberal approach to deciding cases. Only a small minority use the strict construction or historic approach to interpret the Constitution. This departure from the original intent of our Constitution's Founders has given rise over the years to a greatly expanded view of the Constitution and to vast changes in our nation's laws.

III. EXPANSION UNDER THE FOURTEENTH AMENDMENT

Until the Fourteenth Amendment was passed, the guarantees under the Bill of Rights were only applicable against infringements of citizens' rights by the federal government, not by the states. States protected the fundamental rights of their own citizens through their own individual state constitutions and courts. Since the Bill of Rights was originally written for the purpose of protecting the people from the federal government, the states were free to individually determine which of their citizens' rights they would protect. This fact was recognized by the Supreme Court prior to the Civil War in *Barron v. Mayor and City Council of Baltimore* (1833).

Following the Civil War, the Fourteenth Amendment was ratified in 1868 to guarantee that the newly freed slaves in the South would be treated by their state governments in the same way as all other citizens in the state. For that reason, the Fourteenth Amendment guaranteed that no state *"shall make or enforce any law which shall abridge the privileges or immunities of citizens of the United States; nor shall any State deprive any person of life, liberty, or property, without due process of law."* This amendment was never intended to extend all of the individual rights protected by the Bill of Rights to the individual states. Most state constitutions provided for these rights on their own.

Prior to the 1930s, when the common law was still in effect in America, the Supreme Court refused to find the Bill of Rights applicable to the states under the Fourteenth Amendment. Instead, the Court relied on the due process clause of the Fourteenth Amendment to protect individual rights from infringement by the state governments. Today, all of the rights deemed by the Supreme Court to be essential or fundamental to the American scheme of justice have now been made applicable to the states through the Fourteenth Amendment. This includes all of the provisions contained in the First Amendment, Fourth Amendment, Fifth Amendment, Sixth Amendment, and Eighth Amendment.

IV.   EXPANSION UNDER THE COMMERCE CLAUSE

Another avenue under which the power of the federal Constitution has been enlarged to include individual states is through the Court's application of the Commerce Clause. Beginning in 1937, the Court took an entirely different approach to the meaning of this Clause, thereby expanding the power of the Court. One of the key effects of these cases was the denial by the Court that the Tenth Amendment imposed a general limitation on the subjects of federal power.

These changes in the Court's view of the Commerce Clause have greatly affected three areas of litigation: civil rights legislation, federal criminal laws concerning traditionally local crimes, and the regulation of activities of state governmental entities.

The Supreme Court upheld the constitutionality of Title II of the Civil Rights Act of 1964. This law imposed penalties on anyone who deprived another person of equal enjoyment of places of public accommodation on the basis of race, color, religion or national origin. The Supreme Court used the Commerce Clause as the basis for making its decision. Unfortunately, the jurisprudence developed to end the sin of slavery has become not only a mechanism for expanding the power of the federal government, but also for other groups, including homosexuals, to use to achieve ends that are less noble than the goal of granting "life, liberty and happiness" to all of God's children regardless of skin color.

Under the Commerce Clause, Congress may now declare as criminal any activity that either relates to interstate transactions or affects interstate commerce. Also, as has already been demonstrated, any activity that is necessary and proper to regulate in order to effectuate the commerce power can be implemented by Congress to curb criminal activity.

Since 1985, the federal government's regulation of state and local government entities has dramatically changed. The Supreme Court has now refused to recognize that either the Tenth Amendment or the structure of the federal system restricts Congress' power to apply otherwise valid commercial regulations to any state or local governments. This is a reversal of prior case law.

V. EXPANSION UNDER THE APPLICATION OF EVOLUTIONARY PRINCIPLES

In 1859, nearly one hundred years after the publication of William Blackstone's *Commentaries on the Laws of England* (1765), Charles Darwin published his revolutionary book, *The Origin of Species.* While ostensibly a book about biological evolution, philosophical and legal scholars seized on the general theory of evolution as a way to eliminate America's legal dependence on the Creator God of the Bible. Darwin's theory of evolution provided a legal and philosophical, as well as a biological, anchor that could be used to reinterpret life without the need for a Creator Who had the authority to impose His will on His created subjects. That was exactly what some of America's leading jurists were looking for in the late nineteenth century. These jurists wanted to reserve for themselves the right to determine what laws would regulate man's life on earth.

Oliver Wendell Holmes, Jr. was one of those jurists seeking a way to free mankind from the legal constraints imposed by a Creator. As an Associate Justice of the United States Supreme Court in 1917, he wrote a dissenting opinion in which he proclaimed America's independence from Divine law and the nation's right to determine its own law without God, and declared:

> *The common law is not a brooding omnipresence in the sky [based on God], but the articulate voice of some [earthly] sovereign, or quasi sovereign that can be identified.*

Holmes had been arguing since 1887 for the notion that man, not God, should say what the law is. His book on the common law, published that year, was bolstered by the biological elimination of the need for a Creator, as hypothesized by Darwin's theory of evolution.

Holmes and other leading jurists and legal scholars argued throughout the second half of the nineteenth century for a radical new approach to the law, a legal system in which judges would not discover Divine law, but would actually formulate the law themselves by evolving it, case by case, over time. Judges would then be free to move the law in any direction they determined would improve a progressive and evolving society. By the end of the 1930s, the common law was dead in America, having been replaced by statutory law and by the evolving decisions of the Justices of the United States Supreme Court.

Both of these beliefs—the belief in evolution, not creation; and the belief in man, not God—have dominated the teaching of law since the early part of the twentieth century. Before 1900, American lawyers studied the law primarily by reading William Blackstone's book on the common law. The first 140 pages of Blackstone's *Commentaries* outlined the Biblical precepts and principles that controlled English common law. The remainder of the *Commentaries* detailed how this law was being interpreted (not always correctly) in England. For the first hundred years of its existence, America's Founders and, later, its judges and lawyers, used Blackstone's principles in developing the legal system for the newly emerging nation.

After 1870, however, buttressed by Darwin's newly emerging biological theories, legal trendsetters under Dean Christopher Columbus Langdell at the new Harvard Law

School deliberately substituted evolutionary legal principles for the fixed, uniform, and universal laws of God, which the common law and Blackstone's *Commentaries* had previously enshrined in American jurisprudence. Oliver Wendell Holmes, Jr., lauded as a great legal philosopher and jurist of that time, supported this trend and boldly announced that mankind was no longer subordinate to God in the legal arena. These ideas were hailed as a new, modern, legal theory destined to leave behind the religious constraints of the past.

By the beginning of the twentieth century, these elite legal thinkers were intent on undermining the authority of God in American law. They gradually abandoned the Biblical principles memorialized in Blackstone's *Commentaries*, in the Declaration of Independence, in the common law, and in the Constitution. Lawyers began to attend law schools that ignored Blackstone and taught a far-reaching legal theory of evolving case precedents that permitted the law to expand and grow in whatever shape jurists desired.

After this deliberate move away from God, American jurisprudence coasted for quite some time on the collective Biblical memory of the past. But, after the Supreme Court officially abandoned all federal common law based on religion in the 1930s, this memory became increasingly faded and jaded. By the 1960s, American culture began to join the chorus of these legal philosophers and, since then, the God of the Bible that guided and inspired the Founders has been gradually pushed out of America's legal system.

VI.   A DISCONNECTED GENERATION

Whole generations of Americans growing up today have absolutely no idea that the heritage of this country is based on the Bible. Even many adults today have become convinced that America was founded by a group of "separationists" whose primary goal was to create an environment where all public places like schools, courts, and government buildings would be "religion-free zones."

Many Americans today live as if they really believe that the Founding Fathers intended for us to experience both liberty and licentiousness. Many have been led to believe that our Founders would be comfortable with the moral filth and unrighteousness we now live with every day in America. Sometimes it seems that any idea may be expressed in America today except the Truth of the Gospel of Jesus Christ.

During the 1960s, the philosophical worldview of postmodernism became dominant in American higher education, and it was beginning to dominate the courts. These postmodern radical perspectives in worldview and in judicial presuppositions were primarily confined to intellectual circles in the 1960s. Like the good Darwinians they were, a relative handful of philosophical activists, secularist academicians, and judges had successfully moved the American legal system away from God over the course of about ninety years—from the post-Civil War period in the 1870s, when the new system was beginning to be suggested, until the 1960s, when it began to be fully implemented.

Today, as a result of this shift in worldview and jurisprudence, Americans have evolving rights, based not on the absolutes of the Bible, not on the Declaration of Independence, not on the Creator God, but on the state and, primarily, on the whim of judges. For all practical purposes, a postmodern judiciary now determines what rights Americans possess.

America's Founders believed that judges, as well as citizens and politicians, were equally under the authority and, therefore, under the rule of the Law of the Creator. Today, our judicial system has become the cornerstone of a new postmodern America that, since the 1960s, has evolved into a culture many of us no longer recognize or like.

America's legal system has undergone a significant change since the 1960s as the United States Supreme Court, using the evolving case method approach, has taken a decidedly more hostile approach toward Biblical Christianity. This hostility is based on the postmodern presupposition that there is no absolute Truth by which we can guide our lives, either as individuals or as a nation. This is a monumental change from the attitude of our Founding Fathers, who initially based America's government and the rights of its citizens on the absolute sovereignty of God and the absolute Truth of the Bible.

The nineteenth century vision of those like Oliver Wendell Holmes, Jr. and Christopher Columbus Langdell at Harvard Law School has become a twenty-first century reality—the law no longer recognizes a Supreme and Sovereign Creator with the authority to demand obedience from His created subjects. Now judges themselves can decide what is best for society and evolve the law in any direction that furthers their own elitist concepts of societal rights and responsibilities. The Supreme Court has essentially usurped the authority of the Supreme Creator.

CONCLUSION

Time may be short. It is difficult to say just how much longer American Christians will retain the opportunity to make a real change in our culture. This book on the American Constitution was written in an attempt to inform American Christians of the Biblical principles that were responsible for the founding of this great nation and that we must continue to follow if we are to survive as a free people.

We have freedom now in America, but one day it may be lost. God has not given us, or any nation, any guarantees. Our second President, John Adams, once gave a solemn admonition that must be taken seriously in the twenty-first century:

> *Posterity! You will never know how much it cost the present generation to preserve your freedom! I hope you will make good use of it! If you do not, I shall repent it in Heaven that I ever took half the pains to preserve it!*

What is the future of religious liberty in America? Unfortunately, all current indications point to a growing conflict between the faith of Christianity and all branches and levels of American government. There is no doubt that Christians will be in court more and more frequently as new laws increasingly challenge matters relating to the faith.

Consider the following:

As the body of man is knit and kept together in due proportion by the sinews, so every commonwealth is kept and maintained in good order by obedience. But as the sinews are racked and stretched too much, or shrink together too much, it breeds great pain and deformity in a man's body: so if obedience is too much or too little in a commonwealth, it causes much evil and disorder. For too much makes the governors forget their vocation, and to usurp upon their subjects: too little breeds a licentious liberty, and makes the people to forget their duty. And so in both ways the commonwealth grows out of order, and at length comes to havoc and utter destruction.

John Ponet. A Short Treatise on Political Power (1556).

Christians will be forced to take a stand for Christ in our time as never before in American history. But as we take that stand, we must take care to take the right stand, in the right way, and with the right spirit—remembering that even when engaging in Biblically approved disobedience to laws that violate our faith, we are called to promote the eternal agenda that only can be found in God's Word. We Christians must see that our responsibility to government is a responsibility as unto God. That is what Biblical submission to government is truly all about.

Christians in America should not despair. Our hope is in Jesus Christ, and we are merely pilgrims and sojourners in this world. We Christians should be optimistic about the future because we know the One Who holds the future.

Our Constitution still affords us many protections as American Christians. Without a doubt, we enjoy the greatest amount of personal freedom of any nation on earth. We can still spread the Gospel without fear of imprisonment or death, although this right continues to be under attack, particularly by militant gay rights activists who would like to silence all those bringing a Gospel message. We can still choose to educate our children in Christian schools; however, those whose children remain in public schools must stay constantly on the alert to monitor what values they are being taught. We have not yet been forced to adopt an official state religion or non religion; but our most basic religious freedoms are coming under increasing attack today from legislatures, courts, and anti-Christian legal groups.

It has been said that the only thing necessary for evil to triumph is for good men to do nothing, but even good men cannot know what to do if they do not know the source of their liberties. God has granted this nation more than two and a quarter centuries of unparalleled blessings. Today, however, we are seeing the results in our national life of turning our backs on the Biblical God Who gave us liberty.

It is not enough for Christians to know what the Constitution says, although this is vitally important. Neither is it enough merely to champion the guaranteed, God-given rights to which we are entitled. While these actions will slow the pace of the decay that is already sweeping across America and the rest of the world, it will not return our nation to the only true source of her protection—the God of the Bible.

All who know Jesus as Savior must heed the command of II Chronicles 7:14, stated in the Introduction to this book. If we do, God has promised to heal our land. As we examine ourselves and, with the guidance of the Holy Spirit as we first root out the sin in our own lives, we must also remember to pray for those who are in governmental authority over us.

If we do not seek God's face, repent of our sins, and pray for those leaders He has placed in authority over us; if we do not actively participate in our own constitutional government, then we will have only ourselves to blame if the liberties guaranteed in the Declaration of Independence and in the Constitution are taken away from us one by one.

This is a serious message, for this is a serious time. We need to pray for another and for revival in America. The Black Regiment, still preaching from our nation's pulpits, must rally once again to set a righteous standard and to change the hearts and minds of the people. Time may be growing short to bring our Constitution and its interpretation back to its legal roots in the Declaration of Independence and in the Bible.

APPENDIX 1

THE ORIGINAL CONSTITUTION OF THE UNITED STATES OF AMERICA

THE ORIGINAL CONSTITUTION OF THE UNITED STATES OF AMERICA

Preamble

We the People of the United States, in Order to form a more perfect Union, establish Justice, insure domestic Tranquility, provide for the common defence, promote the general Welfare, and secure the Blessings of Liberty to ourselves and our Posterity, do ordain and establish this Constitution for the United States of America.

Article I

Section 1.
All legislative Powers herein granted shall be vested in a Congress of the United States, which shall consist of a Senate and House of Representatives.

Section 2.
The House of Representatives shall be composed of Members chosen every second Year by the People of the several States, and the Electors in each State shall have the Qualifications requisite for Electors of the most numerous Branch of the State Legislature.

No Person shall be a Representative who shall not have attained to the age of twenty five Years, and been seven Years a Citizen of the United States, and who shall not, when elected, be an Inhabitant of that State in which he shall be chosen.

Representatives and direct Taxes shall be apportioned among the several States which may be included within this Union, according to their respective Numbers, which shall be determined by adding to the whole Number of free Persons, including those bound to Service for a Term of Years, and excluding Indians not taxed, three fifths of all other Persons. The actual Enumeration shall be made within three Years after the first Meeting of the Congress of the United States, and within every subsequent Term of ten Years, in such Manner as they shall by Law direct. The Number of Representatives shall not exceed one for every thirty Thousand, but each State shall have at Least one Representative; and until such enumeration shall be made, the State of New Hampshire shall be entitled to chuse three, Massachusetts eight, Rhode-Island and Providence Plantations one, Connecticut five, New-York six, New Jersey four, Pennsylvania eight, Delaware one, Maryland six, Virginia ten, North Carolina five, South Carolina five, and Georgia three.

When vacancies happen in the Representation from any State, the Executive Authority thereof shall issue Writs of Election to fill such Vacancies.

The House of Representatives shall chuse their Speaker and other Officers; and shall have the sole Power of Impeachment.

Section 3.
The Senate of the United States shall be composed of two Senators from each State, chosen by the Legislature thereof, for six Years; and each Senator shall have one Vote.

Immediately after they shall be assembled in Consequence of the first Election, they shall be divided as equally as may be into three Classes. The Seats of the Senators of the first Class shall be vacated at the Expiration of the second Year, of the second Class at the Expiration of the fourth Year, and of the third Class at the Expiration of the sixth Year, so that one third may be chosen every second Year; and if Vacancies happen by Resignation, or otherwise, during the Recess of the Legislature of any State, the Executive thereof may make temporary Appointments until the next Meeting of the Legislature, which shall then fill such Vacancies.

No Person shall be a Senator who shall not have attained to the Age of thirty Years, and been nine Years a Citizen of the United States, and who shall not, when elected, be an Inhabitant of that State for which he shall be chosen.

The Vice President of the United States shall be President of the Senate but shall have no Vote, unless they be equally divided.

The Senate shall chuse their other Officers, and also a President pro tempore, in the Absence of the Vice President, or when he shall exercise the Office of President of the United States.

The Senate shall have the sole Power to try all Impeachments. When sitting for that Purpose, they shall be on Oath or Affirmation. When the President of the United States is tried the Chief Justice shall preside: And no Person shall be convicted without the Concurrence of two thirds of the Members present.

Judgment in Cases of Impeachment shall not extend further than to removal from Office, and disqualification to hold and enjoy any Office of honor, Trust or Profit under the United States: but the Party convicted shall nevertheless be liable and subject to Indictment, Trial, Judgment and Punishment, according to Law.

Section 4.
The Times, Places and Manner of holding Elections for Senators and Representatives, shall be prescribed in each State by the Legislature thereof; but the Congress may at any time by Law make or alter such Regulations, except as to the Places of chusing Senators.

The Congress shall assemble at least once in every Year, and such Meeting shall be on the first Monday in December, unless they shall by Law appoint a different Day.

Section 5.
Each House shall be the Judge of the Elections, Returns and Qualifications of its own Members, and a Majority of each shall constitute a Quorum to do Business; but a smaller Number may adjourn from day to day, and may be authorized to compel the Attendance of absent Members, in such Manner, and under such Penalties as each House may provide.

Each House may determine the Rules of its Proceedings, punish its Members for disorderly Behaviour, and, with the Concurrence of two thirds, expel a Member.

Each House shall keep a Journal of its Proceedings, and from time to time publish the same, excepting such Parts as may in their Judgment require Secrecy; and the Yeas and Nays of the Members of either House on any question shall, at the Desire of one fifth of those Present, be entered on the Journal.

Neither House, during the Session of Congress, shall, without the Consent of the other, adjourn for more than three days, nor to any other Place than that in which the two Houses shall be sitting.

Section 6.
The Senators and Representatives shall receive a Compensation for their Services, to be ascertained by Law, and paid out of the Treasury of the United States. They shall in all Cases, except Treason, Felony and Breach of the Peace, be privileged from Arrest during their Attendance at the Session of their respective Houses, and in going to and returning from the same; and for any Speech or Debate in either House, they shall not be questioned in any other Place.

No Senator or Representative shall, during the Time for which he was elected, be appointed to any civil Office under the Authority of the United States, which shall have been created, or the Emoluments whereof shall have been encreased during such time; and no Person holding any Office under the United States, shall be a Member of either House during his Continuance in Office.

Section 7.
All Bills for raising Revenue shall originate in the House of Representatives; but the Senate may propose or concur with amendments as on other Bills.

Every Bill which shall have passed the House of Representatives and the Senate, shall, before it become a law, be presented to the President of the United States: If he approve he shall sign it, but if not he shall return it, with his Objections to that House in which it shall have originated, who shall enter the Objections at large on their Journal, and proceed to reconsider it. If after such Reconsideration two thirds of that House shall agree to pass the Bill, it shall be sent, together with the Objections, to the other House, by which it shall likewise be reconsidered, and if approved by two thirds of that House, it shall become a Law. But in all such Cases the Votes of both Houses shall be determined by Yeas and Nays, and the Names of the Persons voting for and against the Bill shall be entered on the Journal of each House respectively. If any Bill shall not be returned by the President within ten Days (Sundays excepted) after it shall have been presented to him, the Same shall be a Law, in like Manner as if he had signed it, unless the Congress by their Adjournment prevent its Return, in which Case it shall not be a Law

Every Order, Resolution, or Vote to which the Concurrence of the Senate and House of Representatives may be necessary (except on a question of Adjournment) shall be presented to the President of the United States; and before the Same shall take Effect, shall be approved by him, or being disapproved by him, shall be repassed by two thirds of the Senate and House of Representatives, according to the Rules and Limitations prescribed in the Case of a Bill.

Section 8.
The Congress shall have Power To lay and collect Taxes, Duties, Imposts and Excises, to pay the Debts and provide for the common Defence and general Welfare of the United States; but all Duties, Imposts and Excises shall be uniform throughout the United States;

To borrow Money on the credit of the United States;

To regulate Commerce with foreign Nations, and among the several States, and with the Indian Tribes;

To establish an uniform Rule of Naturalization, and uniform Laws on the subject of Bankruptcies throughout the United States;

To coin Money, regulate the Value thereof, and of foreign Coin, and fix the Standard of Weights and Measures;

To provide for the Punishment of counterfeiting the Securities and current Coin of the United States;

To establish Post Offices and post Roads;

To promote the Progress of Science and useful Arts, by securing for limited Times to Authors and Inventors the exclusive Right to their respective Writings and Discoveries;

To constitute Tribunals inferior to the supreme Court;

To define and punish Piracies and Felonies committed on the high Seas, and Offences against the Law of Nations;

To declare War, grant Letters of Marque and Reprisal, and make Rules concerning Captures on Land and Water;

To raise and support Armies, but no Appropriation of Money to that Use shall be for a longer Term than two Years;

To provide and maintain a Navy;

To make Rules for the Government and Regulation of the land and naval Forces;

To provide for calling forth the Militia to execute the Laws of the Union, suppress Insurrections and repeal Invasions;

To provide for organizing, arming, and disciplining, the Militia, and for governing such Part of them as may be employed in the Service of the United States, reserving to the States respectively, the Appointment of the Officers, and the Authority of training the Militia according to the discipline prescribed by Congress;

To exercise exclusive Legislation in all Cases whatsoever, over such District (not exceeding ten Miles square) as may, by Cession of Particular States, and the Acceptance of Congress, become the Seat of the Government of the United States, and to exercise like Authority over all Places purchased by the Consent of the Legislature of the State in which the Same shall be, for the Erection of Forts, Magazines, Arsenals, dock-Yards and other needful Buildings; —And

To make all Laws which shall be necessary and proper for carrying into Execution the foregoing Powers and all other Powers vested by this Constitution in the Government of the United States, or in any Department or Officer thereof.

Section 9.
The Migration or Importation of such Persons as any of the States now existing shall think proper to admit, shall not be prohibited by the Congress prior to the Year one thousand eight hundred and eight, but a Tax or duty may be imposed on such Importation, not exceeding ten dollars for each Person.

The Privilege of the Writ of Habeas Corpus shall not be suspended, unless when in Cases or Rebellion or Invasion the public Safety may require it.

No Bill of Attainder or ex post facto Law shall be passed.

No Capitation, or other direct, Tax shall be laid, unless in Proportion to the Census of Enumeration herein before directed to be taken.

No Tax or Duty shall be laid on Articles exported from any State.

No Preference shall be given by any Regulation of Commerce or Revenue to the Ports of one State over those of another: nor shall Vessels bound to, or from, one State, be obliged to enter, clear, or pay Duties in another.

No Money shall be drawn from the Treasury, but in Consequence of Appropriations made by Law; and a regular Statement and Account of the Receipts and Expenditures of all public Money shall be published from time to time.

No Title of Nobility shall be granted by the United States: And no Person holding any Office of Profit or Trust under them, shall, without the Consent of the Congress, accept of any present, Emolument, Office, or Title, of any kind whatever, from any King, Prince, or foreign State.

Section 10.
No State shall enter into any Treaty, Alliance, or Confederation; grant Letters of Marque and Reprisal; coin Money; emit Bills of Credit; make any Thing but gold and silver Coin a Tender in Payment of Debts; pass any Bill of Attainder, ex post facto Law, or Law impairing the Obligation of Contracts, or grant any Title of Nobility.

No State shall, without the Consent of the Congress, lay any Imposts or Duties on Imports or Exports, except what may be absolutely necessary for executing it's inspection

Laws: and the net Produce of all Duties and Imposts, laid by any State on Imports or Exports, shall be for the Use of the Treasury of the United States; and all such Laws shall be subject to the Revision and Controul of the Congress.

No State shall, without the Consent of Congress, lay any Duty of Tonnage, keep Troops, or Ships of War in time of Peace, enter into any Agreement or Compact with another State, or with a foreign Power, or engage in War, unless actually invaded, or in such imminent Danger as will not admit of delay.

Article II

Section 1.
The executive Power shall be vested in a President of the United States of America. He shall hold his Office during the Term of four Years, and, together with the Vice President, chosen for the same Term, be elected, as follows:

Each State shall appoint, in such Manner as the Legislature thereof may direct, a Number of Electors, equal to the whole Number of Senators and Representatives to which the State may be entitled in the Congress: but no Senator or Representative, or Person holding an Office of Trust or Profit under the United States, shall be appointed an Elector.

The Electors shall meet in their respective States, and vote by Ballot for two Persons, of whom one at least shall not be an Inhabitant of the same State with themselves. And they shall make a List of all the Persons voted for, and of the Number of Votes for each; which List they shall sign and certify, and transmit sealed to the Seat of the Government of the United States, directed to the President of the Senate. The President of the Senate shall, in the Presence of the

Senate and House of Representatives, open all the Certificates, and the Votes shall then be counted. The Person having the greatest Number of Votes shall be the President, if such Number be a Majority of the whole Number of Electors appointed; and if there be more than one who have such Majority, and have an equal Number of Votes, then the House of Representatives shall immediately chuse by Ballot one of them for President; and if no Person have a Majority, then from the five highest on the List the said House shall in like Manner chuse the President. But in chusing the President, the Votes shall be taken by States, the Representation from each State having one Vote; a quorum for this Purpose shall consist of a Member or Members from two thirds of the States, and a Majority of all the States shall be necessary to a Choice. In every Case, after the Choice of the President, the Person having the greatest Number of Votes of the Electors shall be the Vice President. But if there should remain two or more who have equal Votes, the Senate shall chuse from them by Ballot the Vice President.

The Congress may determine the Time of chusing the Electors, and the Day on which they shall give their Votes; which Day shall be the same throughout the United States.

No Person except a natural born Citizen, or a Citizen of the United States, at the time of the Adoption of this Constitution, shall be eligible to the Office of President; neither shall any person be eligible to that Office who shall not have attained to the Age of thirty five Years, and been fourteen Years a Resident within the United States.

In Case of the Removal of the President from Office, or of his Death, Resignation, or Inability to discharge the Powers and Duties of the said Office, the Same shall devolve on the Vice President, and the Congress may by Law provide for the Case of Removal, Death, Resignation or Inability, both of the President and Vice President, declaring what Officer shall then act as President, and such Officer shall act accordingly, until the Disability be removed, or a President shall be elected.

The President shall, at stated Times, receive for his Services, a Compensation, which shall neither be encreased nor diminished during the Period for which he shall have been elected, and he shall not receive within that Period any other Emolument from the United States, or any of them.

Before he enter on the Execution of his Office, he shall take the following Oath or Affirmation:—"I do solemnly swear (or affirm) that I will faithfully execute the Office of President of the United States, and will to the best of my Ability, preserve, protect and defend the Constitution of the United States."

Section 2.
The President shall be Commander in Chief of the Army and Navy of the United States, and of the Militia of the several States, when called into the actual Service of the United States; he may require the Opinion, in writing, of the principal Officer in each of the executive Departments, upon any Subject relating to the Duties of their respective Offices, and he shall have Power to Grant Reprieves and Pardons for Offences against the United States, except in Cases of Impeachment.

He shall have Power, by and with the Advice and Consent of the Senate, to make Treaties, provided two thirds of the Senators present concur; and he shall nominate, and by and with the Advice and Consent of the Senate, shall appoint Ambassadors, other public Ministers and Consuls, Judges of the supreme Court, and all other Officers of the United States, whose Appointments are not herein otherwise provided for, and which shall be established by Law: but the Congress may by Law vest the Appointment of such inferior Officers, as they think proper, in the President alone, in the Courts of Law, or in the Heads of Departments.

The President shall have Power to fill up all Vacancies that may happen during the Recess of the Senate, by granting Commissions which shall expire at the End of their next Session.

Section 3.
He shall from time to time give to the Congress Information of the State of the Union, and recommend to their Consideration such Measures as he shall judge necessary and expedient; he may, on extraordinary Occasions, convene both Houses, or either of them, and in Case of Disagreement between them, with Respect to the Time of Adjournment, he may adjourn them to such Time as he shall think proper; he shall receive Ambassadors and other public Ministers; he shall take Care that the Laws be faithfully executed, and shall Commission all the Officers of the United States.

Section 4.
The President, Vice President and all civil Officers of the United States, shall be removed from Office on Impeachment for, and Conviction of, Treason, Bribery, or other high Crimes and Misdemeanors.

Article III

Section 1.
The judicial Power of the United States, shall be vested in one supreme Court, and in such inferior Courts as the Congress may from time to time ordain and establish. The Judges, both of the supreme and inferior Courts, shall hold their Offices during good Behaviour, and shall, at stated Times, receive for their Services, a Compensation, which shall not be diminished during their Continuance in Office.

Section 2.
The judicial Power shall extend to all Cases, in Law and Equity, arising under this Constitution, the Laws of the United States, and Treaties made, or which shall be made, under their Authority;—to all Cases affecting Ambassadors, other public Ministers and Consuls;—to all Cases of admiralty and maritime Jurisdiction;—to Controversies to which the United States shall be a Party;—to Controversies between two or more States;—between a State and Citizens of another State;—between Citizens of different States;—between Citizens of the same State claiming Lands under Grants of different States, and between a State, or the Citizens thereof, and foreign States, Citizens or Subjects.

In all Cases affecting Ambassadors, other public Ministers and Consuls, and those in which a State shall be Party, the supreme Court shall have original Jurisdiction. In all the other Cases before mentioned, the supreme Court shall have appellate Jurisdiction, both as to Law and Fact, with such Exceptions, and under such Regulations as the Congress shall make.

The Trial of all Crimes, except in Cases of Impeachment, shall be by Jury; and such Trial shall be held in the State where the said Crimes shall have been committed; but when not committed within any State, the Trial shall be at such Place or Places as the Congress may by Law have directed.

Section 3.

Treason against the United States, shall consist only in levying War against them, or in adhering to their Enemies, giving them Aid and Comfort. No Person shall be convicted of Treason unless on the Testimony of two Witnesses to the same overt Act, or on Confession in open Court.

The Congress shall have Power to declare the Punishment of Treason, but no Attainder of Treason shall work Corruption of Blood, or Forfeiture except during the Life of the Person attainted.

Article IV

Section 1.

Full Faith and Credit shall be given in each State to the public Acts, Records, and judicial Proceedings of every other State. And the Congress may by general Laws prescribe the Manner in which such Acts, Records and Proceedings shall be proved, and the Effect thereof.

Section 2.

The Citizens of each State shall be entitled to all Privileges and Immunities of Citizens in the several States.

A Person charged in any State with Treason, Felony, or other Crime, who shall flee from Justice, and be found in another State, shall on Demand of the executive Authority of the State from which he fled, be delivered up, to be removed to the State having Jurisdiction of the Crime.

No Person held to Service or Labour in one State, under the Laws thereof, escaping into another, shall, in Consequence of any Law or Regulation therein, be discharged from such Service or Labour, but shall be delivered up on Claim of the Party to whom such Service or Labour may be due.

Section 3.
New States may be admitted by the Congress into this Union; but no new State shall be formed or erected within the Jurisdiction of any other State; nor any State be formed by the Junction of two or more States, or Parts of States, without the Consent of the Legislatures of the States concerned as well as of the Congress.

The Congress shall have Power to dispose of and make all needful Rules and Regulations respecting the Territory or other Property belonging to the United States; and nothing in this Constitution shall be so construed as to Prejudice any Claims of the United States, or of any particular State.

Section 4.
The United States shall guarantee to every State in this Union a Republican Form of Government, and shall protect each of them against Invasion; and on Application of the Legislature, or of the Executive (when the Legislature cannot be convened) against domestic Violence.

Article V

The Congress, whenever two thirds of both Houses shall deem it necessary, shall propose Amendments to this Constitution, or, on the Application of the Legislatures of two thirds of the several States, shall call a Convention for proposing Amendments, which, in either Case, shall be valid to all Intents and Purposes, as Part of this

Constitution, when ratified by the Legislatures of three fourths of the several States, or by Conventions in three fourths thereof, as the one or the other Mode of Ratification may be proposed by the Congress; Provided that no Amendment which may be made prior to the Year One thousand eight hundred and eight shall in any Manner affect the first and fourth Clauses in the Ninth Section of the first Article; and that no State, without its Consent, shall be deprived of its equal Suffrage in the Senate.

Article VI

All Debts contracted and Engagements entered into, before the Adoption of this Constitution, shall be as valid against the United States under this Constitution, as under the Confederation.

This Constitution, and the Laws of the United States which shall be made in Pursuance thereof; and all Treaties made, or which shall be made, under the Authority of the United States, shall be the supreme Law of the Land; and the Judges in every State shall be bound thereby, any Thing in the Constitution or Laws of any state to the Contrary notwithstanding.

The Senators and Representatives before mentioned, and the Members of the several State Legislatures, and all executive and judicial Officers, both of the United States and of the several States, shall be bound by Oath or Affirmation, to support this Constitution; but no religious Test shall ever be required as a Qualification to any Office or public Trust under the United States.

Article VII

The Ratification of the Conventions of nine States, shall be sufficient for the Establishment of this Constitution between the States so ratifying the same.

Done in Convention, by the unanimous consent of the States present, the seventeenth day of September, in the year of our Lord one thousand seven hundred and eighty-seven, and of the Independence of the United States of America the twelfth. In witness whereof, we have hereunto subscribed our names.

GEORGE WASHINGTON, President, (and Deputy from *Virginia.*)

New-Hampshire. John Langdon, Nicholas Gilman.

Massachusetts. Nathaniel Gorham, Rufus King.

Connecticut. William Samuel Johnson, Roger Sherman.

New York. Alexander Hamilton.

New Jersey. William Livingston, David Brearley, William Paterson, Jonathan Dayton.

Pennsylvania. Benjamin Franklin, Thomas Mifflin, Robert Morris, George Clymer, Thomas Fitzsimons, Jared Ingersoll, James Wilson, Gouverneur Morris.

Delaware. George Read, Gunning Bedford, jun. John Dickenson, Richard Bassett, Jacob Broom.

Maryland. James M'Henry, Daniel of St. Tho. Jenifer, Daniel Carrol.

Virginia. John Blair, James Madison, jun.

North Carolina. William Blount, Richard Dobbs Spaight, Hugh Williamson.

South Carolina. John Rutledge, Charles Cotesworth Pinckney, Charles Pinckney, Pierce Butler.

Georgia. William Few, Abraham Baldwin.

In Convention Monday, September 17th 1787. Present The States of New Hampshire, Massachusetts, Connecticut, Mr. Hamilton from New York, New Jersey, Pennsylvania, Delaware, Maryland, Virginia, North Carolina, South Carolina and Georgia.

Resolved,

That the preceeding Constitution be laid before the United States in Congress assembled, and that it is the Opinion of this Convention, that it should afterwards be submitted to a Convention of Delegates, chosen in each State by the People thereof, under the Recommendation of its Legislature, for their Assent and Ratification; and that each Convention assenting to, and ratifying the Same, should give Notice thereof to the United States in Congress assembled.

Resolved,

That it is the Opinion of this Convention, that as soon as the Conventions of nine States shall have ratified this Constitution, the United States in Congress assembled should fix a Day on which Electors should be appointed by the States which shall have ratified the same, and a Day on which the Electors should assemble to vote for the President, and the Time and Place for commencing Proceedings under this Constitution. That after such Publication the Electors should be appointed, and the Senators and Representatives elected: That the Electors should meet on the Day fixed for the Election of the President, and should transmit their Votes certified, signed, sealed and directed, as the Constitution requires, to the Secretary of the United States in Congress assembled, that the Senators and Representatives should convene at the Time and Place assigned; that the Senators should appoint a

President of the Senate, for the sole Purpose of receiving, opening and counting the Votes for President; and, that after he shall be chosen, the Congress, together with the President, should, without Delay, proceed to execute this Constitution.

By the Unanimous Order of the Convention

Go: Washington, *President*
W. Jackson, *Secretary*

THE AMENDMENTS TO THE CONSTITUTION OF THE UNITED STATES OF AMERICA

AMENDMENTS TO THE CONSTITUTION OF THE UNITED STATES OF AMERICA

Articles in addition to, and amendment of, the Constitution of the United States of America, proposed by Congress, and ratified by the Legislatures of the several states, pursuant to the Fifth Article of the original Constitution.[i]

Amendment I[ii]

Congress shall make no law respecting an establishment of religion, or prohibiting the free exercise thereof; or abridging the freedom of speech, or of the press; or the right of the people peaceably to assemble, and to petition the Government for a redress of grievances.

Amendment II

A well regulated Militia, being necessary to the security of a free State, the right of the people to keep and bear Arms, shall not be infringed.

Amendment III

No Soldier shall, in time of peace be quartered in any house, without the consent of the Owner, nor in time of war, but in a manner to be prescribed by law.

Amendment IV

The right of the people to be secure in their persons, houses, papers, and effects, against unreasonable searches and seizures, shall not be violated, and no Warrants shall issue, but upon probable cause, supported by Oath or affirmation, and particularly describing the place to be searched, and the persons or things to be seized.

Amendment V

No person shall be held to answer for a capital, or otherwise infamous crime, unless on a presentment or indictment of a Grand Jury, except in cases arising in the land or naval forces, or in the Militia, when in actual service in time of War or public danger; nor shall any person be subject for the same offence to be twice put in jeopardy of life or limb; nor shall be compelled in any criminal case to be a witness against himself, nor be deprived of life, liberty, or property, without due process of law; nor shall private property be taken for public use, without just compensation.

Amendment VI

In all criminal prosecutions, the accused shall enjoy the right to a speedy and public trial, by an impartial jury of the State and district wherein the crime shall have been committed, which district shall have been previously ascertained by law, and to be informed of the nature and cause of the accusation; to be confronted with the witnesses against him; to have compulsory process for obtaining witnesses in his favor, and to have the Assistance of Counsel for his defence.

Amendment VII

In Suits at common law, where the value in controversy shall exceed twenty dollars, the right of trial by jury shall be preserved, and no fact tried by a jury, shall be otherwise re-examined in any Court of the United States, than according to the rules of the common law.

Amendment VIII

Excessive bail shall not be required, nor excessive fines imposed, nor cruel and unusual punishments inflicted.

Amendment IX

The enumeration in the Constitution, of certain rights, shall not be construed to deny or disparage others retained by the people.

Amendment X

The powers not delegated to the United States by the Constitution, nor prohibited by it to the States, are reserved to the States respectively, or to the people.

Amendment XI[iii]

The Judicial power of the United States shall not be construed to extend to any suit in law or equity, commenced or prosecuted against one of the United States by Citizens of another State, or by Citizens or Subjects of any Foreign State.

Amendment XII[iv]

The Electors shall meet in their respective states and vote by ballot for President and Vice-President, one of whom, at least, shall not be an inhabitant of the same state with themselves; they shall name in their ballots the person voted for as President, and in distinct ballots the person voted for as Vice- President, and they shall make distinct lists of all persons voted for as President, and of all persons voted for as Vice-President, and of the number of votes for each, which lists they shall sign and certify, and transmit sealed to the seat of the government of the United States, directed to the President of the Senate;—The President of the Senate shall, in the presence of the Senate and House of Representatives, open all the certificates and the votes shall then be counted;—The person having the greatest Number of votes for President, shall be the President, if such number be a majority of the whole number of Electors appointed; and if no person have such majority, then from the persons having the highest numbers not exceeding three on the list of those voted for as President, the House of Representatives shall choose immediately, by ballot, the President. But in choosing the President, the votes shall be taken by states, the representation from each state having one vote; a quorum for this purpose shall consist of a member or members from two-thirds of the states, and a majority of all the states shall be necessary to a choice. And if the House of Representatives shall not choose a President whenever the right of choice shall devolve upon them, before the fourth day of March next following, then the Vice- President shall act as President, as in the case of the death or other constitutional disability of the President— The person having the greatest number of votes as Vice-President, shall be the Vice-President, if such number be a majority of the whole number of Electors appointed, and if no person have a majority, then from the two highest numbers on the list, the Senate shall choose the Vice-President; a quorum for the purpose shall consist of two-thirds of the whole number of Senators, and a majority of the whole number shall be necessary to a choice. But no person constitutionally ineligible to the office of President shall be eligible to that of Vice-President of the United States.

Amendment XIII [v]

Section 1.
Neither slavery nor involuntary servitude, except as a punishment for crime whereof the party shall have been duly convicted, shall exist within the United States, or any place subject to their jurisdiction.

Section 2.
Congress shall have power to enforce this article by appropriate legislation.

Amendment XIV[vi]

Section. 1.
All persons born or naturalized in the United States and subject to the jurisdiction thereof, are citizens of the United

States and of the State wherein they reside. No State shall make or enforce any law which shall abridge the privileges or immunities of citizens of the United States; nor shall any State deprive any person of life, liberty, or property, without due process of law; nor deny to any person within its jurisdiction the equal protection of the laws.

Section. 2.

Representatives shall be apportioned among the several States according to their respective numbers, counting the whole number of persons in each State, excluding Indians not taxed. But when the right to vote at any election for the choice of electors for President and Vice President of the United States, Representatives in Congress, the Executive and Judicial officers of a State, or the members of the Legislature thereof, is denied to any of the male inhabitants of such State, being twenty-one years of age, and citizens of the United States, or in any way abridged, except for participation in rebellion, or other crime, the basis of representation therein shall be reduced in the proportion which the number of such male citizens shall bear to the whole number of male citizens twenty-one years of age in such State.

Section. 3.

No person shall be a Senator or Representative in Congress, or elector of President and Vice President, or hold any office, civil or military, under the United States, or under any State, who, having previously taken an oath, as a member of Congress, or as an officer of the United States, or as a member of any State legislature, or as an executive or judicial officer of any State, to support the Constitution of the United States, shall have engaged in insurrection or rebellion against the same, or given aid or comfort to the enemies thereof. But Congress may by a vote of two-thirds of each House, remove such disability.

Section. 4.

The validity of the public debt of the United States, authorized by law, including debts incurred for payment of pensions and bounties for services in suppressing insurrection or rebellion, shall not be questioned. But neither the United States nor any State shall assume or pay any debt or obligation incurred in aid of insurrection or rebellion against the United States, or any claim for the loss or emancipation of any slave; but all such debts, obligations and claims shall be held illegal and void.

Section. 5.

The Congress shall have power to enforce, by appropriate legislation, the provisions of this article.

Amendment XV[vii]

Section. 1.

The right of citizens of the United States to vote shall not be denied or abridged by the United States or by any State on account of race, color, or previous condition of servitude.

Section. 2.

The Congress shall have power to enforce this article by appropriate legislation.

Amendment XVI[viii]

The Congress shall have power to lay and collect taxes on incomes, from whatever source derived, without apportionment among the several States, and without regard to any census or enumeration.

Amendment XVII[ix]

The Senate of the United States shall be composed of two Senators from each State, elected by the people thereof, for six years; and each Senator shall have one vote. The electors in each State shall have the qualifications requisite for electors of the most numerous branch of the State legislatures.

When vacancies happen in the representation of any State in the Senate, the executive authority of such State shall issue writs of election to fill such vacancies: Provided, That the legislature of any State may empower the executive thereof to make temporary appointments until the people fill the vacancies by election as the legislature may direct.

This amendment shall not be so construed as to affect the election or term of any Senator chosen before it becomes valid as part of the Constitution.

Amendment XVIII[x]

Section. 1.
After one year from the ratification of this article the manufacture, sale, or transportation of intoxicating liquors within, the importation thereof into, or the exportation thereof from the United States and all territory subject to the jurisdiction thereof for beverage purposes is hereby prohibited.

Sec. 2.
The Congress and the several States shall have concurrent power to enforce this article by appropriate legislation.

Sec. 3.
This article shall be inoperative unless it shall have been ratified as an amendment to the Constitution by the legislatures of the several States, as provided in the Constitution, within seven years from the date of the submission hereof to the States by the Congress.

Amendment XIX[xi]

The right of citizens of the United States to vote shall not be denied or abridged by the United States or by any State on account of sex. Congress shall have power to enforce this article by appropriate legislation.

Amendment XX[xii]

Section. 1.
The terms of the President and Vice President shall end at noon on the 20th day of January, and the terms of Senators and Representatives at noon on the 3d day of January, of the years in which such terms would have ended if this article had not been ratified; and the terms of their successors shall then begin.

Sec. 2.
The Congress shall assemble at least once in every year, and such meeting shall begin at noon on the 3d day of January, unless they shall by law appoint a different day.

Sec. 3.
If, at the time fixed for the beginning of the term of the President, the President elect shall have died, the Vice President elect shall become President. If a President shall not have been chosen before the time fixed for the

beginning of his term, or if the President elect shall have failed to qualify, then the Vice President elect shall act as President until a President shall have qualified; and the Congress may by law provide for the case wherein neither a President elect nor a Vice President elect shall have qualified, declaring who shall then act as President, or the manner in which one who is to act shall be selected, and such person shall act accordingly until a President or Vice President shall have qualified.

Sec. 4.
The Congress may by law provide for the case of the death of any of the persons from whom the House of Representatives may choose a President whenever the right of choice shall have devolved upon them, and for the case of the death of any of the persons from whom the Senate may choose a Vice President whenever the right of choice shall have devolved upon them.

Sec. 5.
Sections 1 and 2 shall take effect on the 15th day of October following the ratification of this article.

Sec. 6.
This article shall be inoperative unless it shall have been ratified as an amendment to the Constitution by the legislatures of three-fourths of the several States within seven years from the date of its submission.

Amendment XXI[xiii]

Section. 1.
The eighteenth article of amendment to the Constitution of the United States is hereby repealed.

Sec. 2.

The transportation or importation into any State, Territory, or possession of the United States for delivery or use therein of intoxicating liquors, in violation of the laws thereof, is hereby prohibited.

Sec. 3.

This article shall be inoperative unless it shall have been ratified as an amendment to the Constitution by conventions in the several States, as provided in the Constitution, within seven years from the date of the submission hereof to the States by the Congress.

Amendment XXII[xiv]

Section. 1.

No person shall be elected to the office of the President more than twice, and no person who has held the office of President, or acted as President, for more than two years of a term to which some other person was elected President shall be elected to the office of the President more than once. But this Article shall not apply to any person holding the office of President, when this Article was proposed by the Congress, and shall not prevent any person who may be holding the office of President, or acting as President, during the term within which this Article becomes operative from holding the office of President or acting as President during the remainder of such term.

Sec. 2.

This article shall be inoperative unless it shall have been ratified as an amendment to the Constitution by the legislatures of three-fourths of the several States within seven years from the date of its submission to the States by the Congress.

Amendment XXIII[xv]

Section. 1.
The District constituting the seat of Government of the United States shall appoint in such manner as the Congress may direct: A number of electors of President and Vice President equal to the whole number of Senators and Representatives in Congress to which the District would be entitled if it were a State, but in no event more than the least populous State; they shall be in addition to those appointed by the States, but they shall be considered, for the purposes of the election of President and Vice President, to be electors appointed by a State; and they shall meet in the District and perform such duties as provided by the twelfth article of amendment.

Sec. 2.
The Congress shall have power to enforce this article by appropriate legislation.

Amendment XXIV[xvi]

Section. 1.
The right of citizens of the United States to vote in any primary or other election for President or Vice President, for electors for President or Vice President, or for Senator or Representative in Congress, shall not be denied or abridged by the United States or any State by reason of failure to pay any poll tax or other tax.

Section. 2.
The Congress shall have power to enforce this article by appropriate legislation.

Amendment XXV[xvii]

Section. 1.

In case of the removal of the President from office or of his death or resignation, the Vice President shall become President.

Section. 2.

Whenever there is a vacancy in the office of the Vice President, the President shall nominate a Vice President who shall take office upon confirmation by a majority vote of both Houses of Congress.

Section. 3.

Whenever the President transmits to the President pro tempore of the Senate and the Speaker of the House of Representatives his written declaration that he is unable to discharge the powers and duties of his office, and until he transmits to them a written declaration to the contrary, such powers and duties shall be discharged by the Vice President as Acting President.

Section. 4.

Whenever the Vice President and a majority of either the principal officers of the executive departments or of such other body as Congress may by law provide, transmit to the President pro tempore of the Senate and the Speaker of the House of Representatives their written declaration that the President is unable to discharge the powers and duties of his office, the Vice President shall immediately assume the powers and duties of the office as Acting President.

Thereafter, when the President transmits to the President pro tempore of the Senate and the Speaker of the House of Representatives his written declaration that no inability exists, he shall resume the powers and duties of his office unless the Vice President and a majority of either the principal officers of the executive department or of such other body as Congress may by law provide, transmit within four days to the President pro tempore of the Senate and the Speaker of the House of Representatives their written declaration that the President is unable to discharge the powers and duties of his office. Thereupon Congress shall decide the issue, assembling within forty-eight hours for that purpose if not in session. If the Congress, within twenty-one days after receipt of the latter written declaration, or, if Congress is not in session, within twenty-one days after Congress is required to assemble, determines by two-thirds vote of both Houses that the President is unable to discharge the powers and duties of his office, the Vice President shall continue to discharge the same as Acting President; otherwise, the President shall resume the powers and duties of his office.

Amendment XXVI[xviii]

Section. 1.
The right of citizens of the United States, who are eighteen years of age or older, to vote shall not be denied or abridged by the United States or by any State on account of age.

Section. 2.
The Congress shall have power to enforce this article by appropriate legislation.

Amendment XXVII[xix]

No law varying the compensation for the services of the Senators and Representatives shall take effect, until an election of Representatives shall have intervened.

---

[i] *These footnotes are provided by the United States Senate on the United States Government Printing Office. No copyright claim is made with respect to original U.S. Government works.*

In Dillon v. Gloss, 256 U.S. 368 (1921), the Supreme Court stated that it would take judicial notice of the date on which a State ratified a proposed constitutional amendment. Accordingly the Court consulted the State journals to determine the dates on which each house of the legislature of certain States ratified the Eighteenth Amendment. It, therefore, follows that the date on which the governor approved the ratification, or the date on which the secretary of state of a given State certified the ratification, or the date on which the Secretary of State of the United States received a copy of said certificate, or the date on which he proclaimed that the amendment had been ratified are not controlling. Hence, the ratification date given in the following notes is the date on which the legislature of a given State approved the particular amendment (signature by the speaker or presiding officers of both houses being considered a part of the ratification of the "legislature"). When that date is not available, the date given is that on which it was approved by the governor or certified by the secretary of state of the particular State. In each case such fact has been noted. Except as otherwise indicated information as to ratification is based on data supplied by the Department of State.

[ii] Brackets enclosing an amendment number indicate that the number was not specifically assigned in the resolution proposing the amendment. It will be seen, accordingly, that only the Thirteenth, Fourteenth, Fifteenth, and Sixteenth Amendments were thus technically ratified by number. The first ten amendments along with two others that were not ratified were proposed by Congress on September 25, 1789, when they passed the Senate, having previously passed the House on September 24 (1 Annals of Congress 88, 913). They appear officially in 1 Stat. 97. Ratification was completed on December 15, 1791, when the eleventh State (Virginia) approved these amendments, there being then 14 States in the Union.

The several state legislatures ratified the first ten amendments to the Constitution on the following dates: New Jersey, November 20, 1789; Maryland, December 19, 1789; North Carolina, December 22, 1789; South Carolina, January 19, 1790; New Hampshire, January 25, 1790; Delaware, January 28, 1790; New York, February 27, 1790; Pennsylvania, March 10, 1790; Rhode Island, June 7, 1790; Vermont, November 3, 1791; Virginia, December 15, 1791. The two amendments that then failed of ratification prescribed the ratio of representation to population in the House, and specified that no law varying the compensation of members of Congress should be effective until after an intervening election of Representatives. The first was ratified by ten States (one short of the requisite number) and the second, by six States; subsequently, this second proposal was taken up by the States in the period 1980-1992 and was proclaimed as ratified as of May 7, 1992. Connecticut, Georgia, and Massachusetts ratified the first ten amendments in 1939.

[iii] The Eleventh Amendment was proposed by Congress on March 4, 1794, when it passed the House, 4 Annals of Congress 477, 478, having previously passed the Senate on January 14, Id., 30, 31. It appears officially in 1 Stat. 402. Ratification was completed on February 7, 1795, when the twelfth State (North Carolina) approved the amendment, there being then 15 States in the Union. Official announcement of ratification was not made until January 8, 1798, when President John Adams in a message to Congress stated that the Eleventh Amendment had been adopted by three-fourths of the States and that it "may now be deemed to be a part of the Constitution." In the interim South Carolina had ratified, and Tennessee had been admitted into the Union as the sixteenth State.

The several state legislatures ratified the Eleventh Amendment on the following dates: New York, March 27, 1794; Rhode Island, March 31, 1794; Connecticut, May 8, 1794; New Hampshire, June 16, 1794; Massachusetts, June 26, 1794; Vermont, between October 9 and November 9, 1794; Virginia, November 18, 1794; Georgia, November 29, 1794; Kentucky, December 7, 1794; Maryland, December 26, 1794; Delaware, January 23, 1795; North Carolina, February 7, 1795; South Carolina, December 4, 1797.

[iv] The Twelfth Amendment was proposed by Congress on December 9, 1803, when it passed the House, 13 Annals of Congress 775, 776, having previously passed the Senate on December 2. Id., 209. It was

not signed by the presiding officers of the House and Senate until December 12. It appears officially in 2 Stat. 306. Ratification was probably completed on June 15, 1804, when the legislature of the thirteenth State (New Hampshire) approved the amendment, there being then 17 States in the Union. The Governor of New Hampshire, however, vetoed this act of the legislature on June 20, and the act failed to pass again by two- thirds vote then required by the state constitution. Inasmuch as Article V of the Federal Constitution specifies that amendments shall become effective "when ratified by legislatures of three-fourths of the several States or by conventions in three-fourths thereof," it has been generally believed that an approval or veto by a governor is without significance. If the ratification by New Hampshire be deemed ineffective, then the amendment became operative by Tennessee's ratification on July 27, 1804. On September 25, 1804, in a circular letter to the Governors of the several States, Secretary of State Madison declared the amendment ratified by three-fourths of the States.

The several state legislatures ratified the Twelfth Amendment on the following dates: North Carolina, December 22, 1803; Maryland, December 24, 1803; Kentucky, December 27, 1803; Ohio, between December 5 and December 30, 1803; Virginia, between December 20, 1803 and February 3, 1804; Pennsylvania, January 5, 1804; Vermont, January 30, 1804; New York, February 10, 1804; New Jersey, February 22, 1804; Rhode Island, between February 27 and March 12, 1804; South Carolina, May 15, 1804; Georgia, May 19, 1804; New Hampshire, June 15, 1804; and Tennessee, July 27, 1804. The amendment was rejected by Delaware on January 18, 1804, and by Connecticut at its session begun May 10, 1804. Massachusetts ratified this amendment in 1961.

[v] The Thirteenth Amendment was proposed by Congress on January 31, 1865, when it passed the House, Cong. Globe (38th Cong., 2d Sess.) 531, having previously passed the Senate on April 8, 1964. Id. (38th cong., 1st Sess.), 1940. It appears officially in 13 Stat. 567 under the date of February 1, 1865. Ratification was completed on December 6, 1865, when the legislature of the twenty-seventh State (Georgia) approved the amendment, there being then 36 States in the Union. On December 18, 1865, Secretary of State Seward certified that the Thirteenth Amendment had become a part of the Constitution, 13 Stat. 774.

The several state legislatures ratified the Thirteenth Amendment on the following dates: Illinois, February 1, 1865; Rhode Island, February 2,

1865; Michigan, February 2, 1865; Maryland, February 3, 1865; New York, February 3, 1865; West Virginia, February 3, 1865; Missouri, February 6, 1865; Maine, February 7, 1865; Kansas, February 7, 1865; Massachusetts, February 7, 1865; Pennsylvania, February 8, 1865; Virginia, February 9, 1865; Ohio, February 10, 1865; Louisiana, February 15 or 16, 1865; Indiana, February 16, 1865; Nevada, February 16, 1865; Minnesota, February 23, 1865; Wisconsin, February 24, 1865; Vermont, March 9, 1865 (date on which it was "approved" by Governor); Tennessee, April 7, 1865; Arkansas, April 14, 1865; Connecticut, May 4, 1865; New Hampshire, June 30, 1865; South Carolina, November 13, 1865; Alabama, December 2, 1865 (date on which it was "approved" by Provisional Governor); North Carolina, December 4, 1865; Georgia, December 6, 1865; Oregon, December 11, 1865; California, December 15, 1865; Florida, December 28, 1865 (Florida again ratified this amendment on June 9, 1868, upon its adoption of a new constitution); Iowa, January 17, 1866; New Jersey, January 23, 1866 (after having rejected the amendment on March 16, 1865); Texas, February 17, 1870; Delaware, February 12, 1901 (after having rejected the amendment on February 8, 1865). The amendment was rejected by Kentucky on February 24, 1865, and by Mississippi on December 2, 1865.

[vi] The Fourteenth Amendment was proposed by Congress on June 13, 1866, when it passed the House, Cong. Globe (39th Cong., 1st Sess.) 3148, 3149, having previously passed the Senate on June 8. Id., 3042. It appears officially in 14 Stat. 358 under date of June 16, 1866. Ratification was probably completed on July 9, 1868, when the legislature of the twenty-eighth State (South Carolina or Louisiana) approved the amendment, there being then 37 States in the Union. However, Ohio and New Jersey had prior to that date "withdrawn" their earlier assent to this amendment. Accordingly, Secretary of State Seward on July 20, 1868, certified that the amendment had become a part of the Constitution if the said withdrawals were ineffective. 15 Stat. 706-707. Congress on July 21, 1868, passed a joint resolution declaring the amendment a part of the Constitution and directing the Secretary to promulgate it as such. On July 28, 1868, Secretary Seward certified without reservation that the amendment was a part of the Constitution. In the interim, two other States, Alabama on July 13 and Georgia on July 21, 1868, had added their ratifications.

The several state legislatures ratified the Fourteenth Amendment on the following dates: Connecticut, June 30, 1866; New Hampshire, July 7, 1866; Tennessee, July 19, 1866; New Jersey, September 11, 1866 (the

New Jersey Legislature on February 20, 1868 "withdrew" its consent to the ratification; the Governor vetoed that bill on March 5, 1868; and it was repassed over his veto on March 24, 1868); Oregon, September 19, 1866 (Oregon "withdrew" its consent on October 15, 1868); Vermont, October 30, 1866; New York, January 10, 1867; Ohio, January 11, 1867 (Ohio "withdrew" its consent on January 15, 1868); Illinois, January 15, 1867; West Virginia, January 16, 1867; Michigan, January 16, 1867; Kansas, January 17, 1867; Minnesota, January 17, 1867; Maine, January 19, 1867; Nevada, January 22, 1867; Indiana, January 23, 1867; Missouri, January 26, 1867 (date on which it was certified by the Missouri secretary of state); Rhode Island, February 7, 1867; Pennsylvania, February 12, 1867; Wisconsin, February 13, 1867 (actually passed February 7, but not signed by legislative officers until February 13); Massachusetts, March 20, 1867; Nebraska, June 15, 1867; Iowa, March 9, 1868; Arkansas, April 6, 1868; Florida, June 9, 1868; North Carolina, July 2, 1868 (after having rejected the amendment on December 13, 1866); Louisiana, July 9, 1868 (after having rejected the amendment on February 6, 1867); South Carolina, July 8, 1868 (after having rejected the amendment on December 20, 1866); Alabama, July 13, 1868 (date on which it was "approved" by the Governor); Georgia, July 21, 1868 (after having rejected the amendment on November 9, 1866—Georgia ratified again on February 2, 1870); Virginia, October 8, 1869 (after having rejected the amendment on January 9, 1867); Mississippi, January 17, 1870; Texas, February 18, 1870 (after having rejected the amendment on October 27, 1866); Delaware, February 12, 1901 (after having rejected the amendment on February 7, 1867). The amendment was rejected (and not subsequently ratified) by Kentucky on January 8, 1867. Maryland and California ratified this amendment in 1959.

[vii] The Fifteenth Amendment was proposed by Congress on February 26, 1869, when it passed the Senate, Cong. Globe (40th Cong., 3rd Sess.) 1641, having previously passed the House on February 25. Id., 1563, 1564. It appears officially in 15 Stat. 346 under the date of February 27, 1869. Ratification was probably completed on February 3, 1870, when the legislature of the twenty-eighth State (Iowa) approved the amendment, there being then 37 States in the Union. However, New York had prior to that date "withdrawn" its earlier assent to this amendment. Even if this withdrawal were effective, Nebraska's ratification on February 17, 1870, authorized Secretary of State Fish's certification of March 30, 1870, that the Fifteenth Amendment had become a part of the Constitution. 16 Stat. 1131.

The several state legislatures ratified the Fifteenth Amendment on the following dates: Nevada, March 1, 1869; West Virginia, March 3, 1869; North Carolina, March 5, 1869; Louisiana, March 5, 1869 (date on which it was "approved" by the Governor); Illinois, March 5, 1869; Michigan, March 5, 1869; Wisconsin, March 5, 1869; Maine, March 11, 1869; Massachusetts, March 12, 1869; South Carolina, March 15, 1869; Arkansas, March 15, 1869; Pennsylvania, March 25, 1869; New York, April 14, 1869 (New York "withdrew" its consent to the ratification on January 5, 1870); Indiana, May 14, 1869; Connecticut, May 19, 1869; Florida, June 14, 1869; New Hampshire, July 1, 1869; Virginia, October 8, 1869; Vermont, October 20, 1869; Alabama, November 16, 1869; Missouri, January 7, 1870 (Missouri had ratified the first section of the 15th Amendment on March 1, 1869; it failed to include in its ratification the second section of the amendment); Minnesota, January 13, 1870; Mississippi, January 17, 1870; Rhode Island, January 18, 1870; Kansas, January 19, 1870 (Kansas had by a defectively worded resolution previously ratified this amendment on February 27, 1869); Ohio, January 27, 1870 (after having rejected the amendment on May 4, 1869); Georgia, February 2, 1870; Iowa, February 3, 1870; Nebraska, February 17, 1870; Texas, February 18, 1870; New Jersey, February 15, 1871 (after having rejected the amendment on February 7, 1870); Delaware, February 12, 1901 (date on which approved by Governor; Delaware had previously rejected the amendment on March 18, 1869). The amendment was rejected (and not subsequently ratified) by Kentucky, Maryland, and Tennessee. California ratified this amendment in 1962 and Oregon in 1959.

viii The Sixteenth Amendment was proposed by Congress on July 12, 1909, when it passed the House, 44 Cong. Rec. (61st Cong., 1st Sess.) 4390, 4440, 4441, having previously passed the Senate on July 5. Id., 4121. It appears officially in 36 Stat. 184. Ratification was completed on February 3, 1913, when the legislature of the thirty-sixth State (Delaware, Wyoming, or New Mexico) approved the amendment, there being then 48 States in the Union. On February 25, 1913, Secretary of State Knox certified that this amendment had become a part of the Constitution. 37 Stat. 1785.

The several state legislatures ratified the Sixteenth Amendment on the following dates: Alabama, August 10, 1909; Kentucky, February 8, 1910; South Carolina, February 19, 1910; Illinois, March 1, 1910; Mississippi, March 7, 1910; Oklahoma, March 10, 1910; Maryland, April 8, 1910; Georgia, August 3, 1910; Texas, August 16, 1910; Ohio, January 19, 1911; Idaho, January 20, 1911; Oregon, January 23, 1911;

Washington, January 26, 1911; Montana, January 27, 1911; Indiana, January 30, 1911; California, January 31, 1911; Nevada, January 31, 1911; South Dakota, February 1, 1911; Nebraska, February 9, 1911; North Carolina, February 11, 1911; Colorado, February 15, 1911; North Dakota, February 17, 1911; Michigan, February 23, 1911; Iowa, February 24, 1911; Kansas, March 2, 1911; Missouri, March 16, 1911; Maine, March 31, 1911; Tennessee, April 7, 1911; Arkansas, April 22, 1911 (after having rejected the amendment at the session begun January 9, 1911); Wisconsin, May 16, 1911; New York, July 12, 1911; Arizona, April 3, 1912; Minnesota, June 11, 1912; Louisiana, June 28, 1912; West Virginia, January 31, 1913; Delaware, February 3, 1913; Wyoming, February 3, 1913; New Mexico, February 3, 1913; New Jersey, February 4, 1913; Vermont, February 19, 1913; Massachusetts, March 4, 1913; New Hampshire, March 7, 1913 (after having rejected the amendment on March 2, 1911). The amendment was rejected (and not subsequently ratified) by Connecticut, Rhode Island, and Utah.

[ix] The Seventeenth Amendment was proposed by Congress on May 13, 1912, when it passed the House, 48 Cong. Rec. (62d Cong., 2d Sess.) 6367, having previously passed the Senate on June 12, 1911. 47 Cong. Rec. (62d Cong., 1st Sess.) 1925. It appears officially in 37 Stat. 646. Ratification was completed on April 8, 1913, when the thirty-sixth State (Connecticut) approved the amendment, there being then 48 States in the Union. On May 31, 1913, Secretary of State Bryan certified that it had become a part of the Constitution. 38 Stat 2049.

The several state legislatures ratified the Seventeenth Amendment on the following dates: Massachusetts, May 22, 1912; Arizona, June 3, 1912; Minnesota, June 10, 1912; New York, January 15, 1913; Kansas, January 17, 1913; Oregon, January 23, 1913; North Carolina, January 25, 1913; California, January 28, 1913; Michigan, January 28, 1913; Iowa, January 30, 1913; Montana, January 30, 1913; Idaho, January 31, 1913; West Virginia, February 4, 1913; Colorado, February 5, 1913; Nevada, February 6, 1913; Texas, February 7, 1913; Washington, February 7, 1913; Wyoming, February 8, 1913; Arkansas, February 11, 1913; Illinois, February 13, 1913; North Dakota, February 14, 1913; Wisconsin, February 18, 1913; Indiana, February 19, 1913; New Hampshire, February 19, 1913; Vermont, February 19, 1913; South Dakota, February 19, 1913; Maine, February 20, 1913; Oklahoma, February 24, 1913; Ohio, February 25, 1913; Missouri, March 7, 1913; New Mexico, March 13, 1913; Nebraska, March 14, 1913; New Jersey, March 17, 1913; Tennessee, April 1, 1913; Pennsylvania, April 2, 1913; Connecticut, April 8, 1913; Louisiana, June 5, 1914. The amendment was rejected by Utah on February 26, 1913.

^x The Eighteenth Amendment was proposed by Congress on December 18, 1917, when it passed the Senate, Cong. Rec. (65th Cong. 2d Sess.) 478, having previously passed the House on December 17. Id., 470. It appears officially in 40 Stat. 1059. Ratification was completed on January 16, 1919, when the thirty-sixth State approved the amendment, there being then 48 States in the Union. On January 29, 1919, Acting Secretary of State Polk certified that this amendment had been adopted by the requisite number of States. 40 Stat. 1941. By its terms this amendment did not become effective until 1 year after ratification.

The several state legislatures ratified the Eighteenth Amendment on the following dates: Mississippi, January 8, 1918; Virginia, January 11, 1918; Kentucky, January 14, 1918; North Dakota, January 28, 1918 (date on which approved by Governor); South Carolina, January 29, 1918; Maryland, February 13, 1918; Montana, February 19, 1918; Texas, March 4, 1918; Delaware, March 18, 1918; South Dakota, March 20, 1918; Massachusetts, April 2, 1918; Arizona, May 24, 1918; Georgia, June 26, 1918; Louisiana, August 9, 1918 (date on which approved by Governor); Florida, November 27, 1918; Michigan, January 2, 1919; Ohio, January 7, 1919; Oklahoma, January 7, 1919; Idaho, January 8, 1919; Maine, January 8, 1919; West Virginia, January 9, 1919; California, January 13, 1919; Tennessee, January 13, 1919; Washington, January 13, 1919; Arkansas, January 14, 1919; Kansas, January 14, 1919; Illinois, January 14, 1919; Indiana, January 14, 1919; Alabama, January 15, 1919; Colorado, January 15, 1919; Iowa, January 15, 1919; New Hampshire, January 15, 1919; Oregon, January 15, 1919; Nebraska, January 16, 1919; North Carolina, January 16, 1919; Utah, January 16, 1919; Missouri, January 16, 1919; Wyoming, January 16, 1919; Minnesota, January 17, 1919; Wisconsin, January 17, 1919; New Mexico, January 20, 1919; Nevada, January 21, 1919; Pennsylvania, February 25, 1919; Connecticut, May 6, 1919; New Jersey, March 9, 1922; New York, January 29, 1919; Vermont, January 29, 1919.

^{xi} The Nineteenth Amendment was proposed by Congress on June 4, 1919, when it passed the Senate, Cong. Rec. (66th Cong., 1st Sess.) 635, having previously passed the house on May 21. Id., 94. It appears officially in 41 Stat. 362. Ratification was completed on August 18, 1920, when the thirty-sixth State (Tennessee) approved the amendment, there being then 48 States in the Union. On August 26, 1920, Secretary

of Colby certified that it had become a part of the Constitution. 41 Stat. 1823.

The several state legislatures ratified the Nineteenth Amendment on the following dates: Illinois, June 10, 1919 (readopted June 17, 1919); Michigan, June 10, 1919; Wisconsin, June 10, 1919; Kansas, June 16, 1919; New York, June 16, 1919; Ohio, June 16, 1919; Pennsylvania, June 24, 1919; Massachusetts, June 25, 1919; Texas, June 28, 1919; Iowa, July 2, 1919 (date on which approved by Governor); Missouri, July 3, 1919; Arkansas, July 28, 1919; Montana, August 2, 1919 (date on which approved by governor); Nebraska, August 2, 1919; Minnesota, September 8, 1919; New Hampshire, September 10, 1919 (date on which approved by Governor); Utah, October 2, 1919; California, November 1, 1919; Maine, November 5, 1919; North Dakota, December 1, 1919; South Dakota, December 4, 1919 (date on which certified); Colorado, December 15, 1919 (date on which approved by Governor); Kentucky, January 6, 1920; Rhode Island, January 6, 1920; Oregon, January 13, 1920; Indiana, January 16, 1920; Wyoming, January 27, 1920; Nevada, February 7, 1920; New Jersey, February 9, 1920; Idaho, February 11, 1920; Arizona, February 12, 1920; New Mexico, February 21, 1920 (date on which approved by govrnor); Oklahoma, February 28, 1920; West Virginia, March 10, 1920 (confirmed September 21, 1920); Vermont, February 8, 1921. The amendment was rejected by Georgia on July 24, 1919; by Alabama on September 22, 1919; by South Carolina on January 29, 1920; by Virginia on February 12, 1920; by Maryland on February 24, 1920; by Mississippi on March 29, 1920; by Louisiana on July 1, 1920. This amendment was subsequently ratified by Virginia in 1952, Alabama in 1953, Florida in 1969, and Georgia and Louisiana in 1970.

[xii] The Twentieth Amendment was proposed by Congress on March 2, 1932, when it passed the Senate, Cong. Rec. (72d Cong., 1st Sess.) 5086, having previously passed the House on March 1. Id., 5027. It appears officially in 47 Stat. 745. Ratification was completed on January 23, 1933, when the thirty-sixth State approved the amendment, there being then 48 States in the Union. On February 6, 1933, Secretary of State Stimson certified that it had become a part of the Constitution. 47 Stat. 2569.

The several state legislatures ratified the Twentieth Amendment on the following dates: Virginia, March 4, 1932; New York, March 11, 1932; Mississippi, March 16, 1932; Arkansas March 17, 1932; Kentucky, March 17, 1932; New Jersey, March 21, 1932; South Carolina, March

25, 1932; Michigan, March 31, 1932; Maine, April 1, 1932; Rhode Island, April 14, 1932; Illinois, April 21, 1932; Louisiana, June 22, 1932; West Virginia, July 30, 1932; Pennsylvania, August 11, 1932; Indiana, August 15, 1932; Texas, September 7, 1932; Alabama, September 13, 1932; California, January 4, 1933; North Carolina, January 5, 1933; North Dakota, January 9, 1933; Minnesota, January 12, 1933; Arizona, January 13, 1933; Montana, January 13, 1933; Nebraska, January 13, 1933; Oklahoma, January 13, 1933; Kansas, January 16, 1933; Oregon, January 16, 1933; Delaware, January 19, 1933; Washington, January 19, 1933; Wyoming, January 19, 1933; Iowa, January 20, 1933; South Dakota, January 20, 1933; Tennessee, January 20, 1933; Idaho, January 21, 1933; New Mexico, January 21, 1933; Georgia, January 23, 1933; Missouri, January 23, 1933; Ohio, January 23, 1933; Utah, January 23, 1933; Colorado, January 24, 1933; Massachusetts, January 24, 1933; Wisconsin, January 24, 1933; Nevada, January 26, 1933; Connecticut, January 27, 1933; New Hampshire, January 31, 1933; Vermont, February 2, 1933; Maryland, March 24, 1933; Florida, April 26, 1933.

[xiii] The Twenty-first Amendment was proposed by Congress on February 20, 1933, when it passed the House, Cong. Rec. (72d Cong., 2d Sess.) 4516, having previously passed the Senate on February 16. Id., 4231. It appears officially in 47 Stat. 1625. Ratification was completed on December 5, 1933, when the thirty-sixth State (Utah) approved the amendment, there being then 48 States in the Union. On December 5, 1933, Acting Secretary of State Phillips certified that it had been adopted by the requisite number of States. 48 Stat. 1749.

The several state conventions ratified the Twenty-first Amendment on the following dates: Michigan, April 10, 1933; Wisconsin, April 25, 1933; Rhode Island, May 8, 1933; Wyoming, May 25, 1933; New Jersey, June 1, 1933; Delaware, June 24, 1933; Indiana, June 26, 1933; Massachusetts, June 26, 1933; New York, June 27, 1933; Illinois, July 10, 1933; Iowa, July 10, 1933; Connecticut, July 11, 1933; New Hampshire, July 11, 1933; California, July 24, 1933; West Virginia, July 25, 1933; Arkansas, August 1, 1933; Oregon, August 7, 1933; Alabama, August 8, 1933; Tennessee, August 11, 1933; Missouri, August 29, 1933; Arizona, September 5, 1933; Nevada, September 5, 1933; Vermont, September 23, 1933; Colorado, September 26, 1933; Washington, October 3, 1933; Minnesota, October 10, 1933; Idaho, October 17, 1933; Maryland, October 18, 1933; Virginia, October 25, 1933; New Mexico, November 2, 1933; Florida, November 14, 1933; Texas, November 24, 1933; Kentucky, November 27, 1933; Ohio, December 5, 1933; Pennsylvania, December 5, 1933; Utah, December

5, 1933; Maine, December 6, 1933; Montana, August 6, 1934. The amendment was rejected by a convention in the State of South Carolina, on December 4, 1933. The electorate of the State of North Carolina voted against holding a convention at a general election held on November 7, 1933.

[xiv] The Twenty-second Amendment was proposed by Congress on March 24, 1947, having passed the House on March 21, 1947, Cong. Rec. (80th Cong., 1st Sess.) 2392, and having previously passed the Senate on March 12, 1947. Id., 1978. It appears officially in 61 Stat. 959. Ratification was completed on February 27, 1951, when the thirty-sixth State (Minnesota) approved the amendment, there being then 48 States in the Union. On March 1, 1951, Jess Larson, Administrator of General Services, certified that it had been adopted by the requisite number of States. 16 Fed. Reg. 2019.

A total of 41 state legislatures ratified the Twenty-second Amendment on the following dates: Maine, March 31, 1947; Michigan, March 31, 1947; Iowa, April 1, 1947; Kansas, April 1, 1947; New Hampshire, April 1, 1947; Delaware, April 2, 1947; Illinois, April 3, 1947; Oregon, April 3, 1947; Colorado, April 12, 1947; California, April 15, 1947; New Jersey, April 15, 1947; Vermont, April 15, 1947; Ohio, April 16, 1947; Wisconsin, April 16, 1947; Pennsylvania, April 29, 1947; Connecticut, May 21, 1947; Missouri, May 22, 1947; Nebraska, May 23, 1947; Virginia, January 28, 1948; Mississippi, February 12, 1948; New York, March 9, 1948; South Dakota, January 21, 1949; North Dakota, February 25, 1949; Louisiana, May 17, 1950; Montana, January 25, 1951; Indiana, January 29, 1951; Idaho, January 30, 1951; New Mexico, February 12, 1951; Wyoming, February 12, 1951; Arkansas, February 15, 1951; Georgia, February 17, 1951; Tennessee, February 20, 1951; Texas, February 22, 1951; Utah, February 26, 1951; Nevada, February 26, 1951; Minnesota, February 27, 1951; North Carolina, February 28, 1951; South Carolina, March 13, 1951; Maryland, March 14, 1951; Florida, April 16, 1951; and Alabama, May 4, 1951.

[xv] The Twenty-third Amendment was proposed by Congress on June 16, 1960, when it passed the Senate, Cong. Rec. (86th Cong., 2d Sess.) 12858, having previously passed the House on June 14. Id., 12571. It appears officially in 74 Stat. 1057. Ratification was completed on March 29, 1961, when the thirty-eighth State (Ohio) approved the amendment, there being then 50 States in the Union. On April 3, 1961,

John L. Moore, Administrator of General Services, certified that it had been adopted by the requisite number of States. 26 Fed. Reg. 2808.

The several state legislatures ratified the Twenty-third Amendment on the following dates: Hawaii, June 23, 1960; Massachusetts, August 22, 1960; New Jersey, December 19, 1960; New York, January 17, 1961; California, January 19, 1961; Oregon, January 27, 1961; Maryland, January 30, 1961; Idaho, January 31, 1961; Maine, January 31, 1961; Minnesota, January 31, 1961; New Mexico, February 1, 1961; Nevada, February 2, 1961; Montana, February 6, 1961; Colorado, February 8, 1961; Washington, February 9, 1961; West Virginia, February 9, 1961; Alaska, February 10, 1961; Wyoming, February 13, 1961; South Dakota, February 14, 1961; Delaware, February 20, 1961; Utah, February 21, 1961; Wisconsin, February 21, 1961; Pennsylvania, February 28, 1961; Indiana, March 3, 1961; North Dakota, March 3, 1961; Tennessee, March 6, 1961; Michigan, March 8, 1961; Connecticut, March 9, 1961; Arizona, March 10, 1961; Illinois, March 14, 1961; Nebraska, March 15, 1961; Vermont, March 15, 1961; Iowa, March 16, 1961; Missouri, March 20, 1961; Oklahoma, March 21, 1961; Rhode Island, March 22, 1961; Kansas, March 29, 1961; Ohio, March 29, 1961, and New Hampshire, March 30, 1961.

[xvi] The Twenty-fourth Amendment was proposed by Congress on September 14, 1962, having passed the House on August 27, 1962. Cong. Rec. (87th Cong., 2d Sess.) 17670 and having previously passed the Senate on March 27, 1962. Id., 5105. It appears officially in 76 Stat. 1259. Ratification was completed on January 23, 1964, when the thirty-eighth State (South Dakota) approved the Amendment, there being then 50 States in the Union. On February 4, 1964, Bernard L. Boutin, Administrator of General Services, certified that it had been adopted by the requisite number of States. 25 Fed. Reg. 1717. President Lyndon B. Johnson signed this certificate.

Thirty-eight state legislatures ratified the Twenty-fourth Amendment on the following dates: Illinois, November 14, 1962; New Jersey, December 3, 1962; Oregon, January 25, 1963; Montana, January 28, 1963; West Virginia, February 1, 1963; New York, February 4, 1963; Maryland, February 6, 1963; California, February 7, 1963; Alaska, February 11, 1963; Rhode Island, February 14, 1963; Indiana, February 19, 1963; Michigan, February 20, 1963; Utah, February 20, 1963; Colorado, February 21, 1963; Minnesota, February 27, 1963; Ohio, February 27, 1963; New Mexico, March 5, 1963; Hawaii, March 6, 1963; North Dakota, March 7, 1963; Idaho, March 8, 1963; Washington, March 14, 1963; Vermont, March 15, 1963; Nevada,

March 19, 1963; Connecticut, March 20, 1963; Tennessee, March 21, 1963; Pennsylvania, March 25, 1963; Wisconsin, March 26, 1963; Kansas, March 28, 1963; Massachusetts, March 28, 1963; Nebraska, April 4, 1963; Florida, April 18, 1963; Iowa, April 24, 1963; Delaware, May 1, 1963; Missouri, May 13, 1963; New Hampshire, June 16, 1963; Kentucky, June 27, 1963; Maine, January 16, 1964; South Dakota, January 23, 1964.

[xvii] This Amendment was proposed by the Eighty-ninth Congress by Senate Joint Resolution No. 1, which was approved by the Senate on February 19, 1965, and by the House of Representatives, in amended form, on April 13, 1965. The House of Representatives agreed to a Conference Report on June 30, 1965, and the Senate agreed to the Conference Report on July 6, 1965. It was declared by the Administrator of General Services, on February 23, 1967, to have been ratified.

This Amendment was ratified by the following States: Nebraska, July 12, 1965; Wisconsin, July 13, 1965; Oklahoma, July 16, 1965; Massachusetts, August 9, 1965; Pennsylvania, August 18, 1965; Kentucky, September 15, 1965; Arizona, September 22, 1965; Michigan, October 5, 1965; Indiana, October 20, 1965; California, October 21, 1965; Arkansas, November 4, 1965; New Jersey, November 29, 1965; Delaware, December 7, 1965; Utah, January 17, 1966; West Virginia, January 20, 1966; Maine, January 24, 1966; Rhode Island, January 28, 1966; Colorado, February 3, 1966; New Mexico, February 3, 1966; Kansas, February 8, 1966; Vermont, February 10, 1966; Alaska, February 18, 1966; Idaho, March 2, 1966; Hawaii, March 3, 1966; Virginia, March 8, 1966; Mississippi, March 10, 1966; New York, March 14, 1966; Maryland, March 23, 1966; Missouri, March 30, 1966; New Hampshire, June 13, 1966; Louisiana, July 5, 1966; Tennessee, January 12, 1967; Wyoming, January 25, 1967; Washington, January 26, 1967; Iowa, January 26, 1967; Oregon, February 2, 1967; Minnesota, February 10, 1967; Nevada, February 10, 1967; Connecticut, February 14, 1967; Montana, February 15, 1967; South Dakota, March 6, 1967; Ohio, March 7, 1967; Alabama, March 14, 1967; North Carolina, March 22, 1967 Illinois, March 22, 1967; Texas, April 25, 1967; Florida, May 25, 1967.

Publication of the certifying statement of the Administrator of General Services that the Amendment had become valid was made on February 25, 1967, F.R. Doc. 67-2208, 32 Fed. Reg. 3287.

^{xviii} The Twenty-sixth Amendment was proposed by Congress on March 23, 1971, upon passage by the House of Representatives, the Senate having previously passed an identical resolution on March 10, 1971. It appears officially in 85 Stat. 825. Ratification was completed on July 1, 1971, when action by the legislature of the 38th State, North Carolina, was concluded, and the Administrator of the General Services Administration officially certified it to have been duly ratified on July 5, 1971. 36 Fed. Reg. 12725.

As of the publication of this volume, 42 States had ratified this Amendment: Connecticut, March 23, 1971; Delaware, March 23, 1971; Minnesota, March 23, 1971; Tennessee, March 23, 1971; Washington, March 23, 1971; Hawaii, March 24, 1971; Massachusetts, March 24, 1971; Montana, March 29, 1971; Arkansas, March 30, 1971; Idaho, March 30, 1971; Iowa, March 30, 1971; Nebraska, April 2, 1971; New Jersey, April 3, 1971; Kansas, April 7, 1971; Michigan, April 7, 1971; Alaska, April 8, 1971; Maryland, April 8, 1971; Indiana, April 8, 1971; Maine, April 9, 1971; Vermont, April 16, 1971; Louisiana, April 17, 1971; California, April 19, 1971; Colorado, April 27, 1971; Pennsylvania, April 27, 1971; Texas, April 27, 1971; South Carolina, April 28, 1971; West Virginia, April 28, 1971; New Hampshire, May 13, 1971; Arizona, May 14, 1971; Rhode Island, May 27, 1971; New York, June 2, 1971; Oregon, June 4, 1971; Missouri, June 14, 1971; Wisconsin, June 22, 1971; Illinois, June 29, 1971; Alabama, June 30, 1971; Ohio, June 30, 1971; North Carolina, July 1, 1971; Oklahoma, July 1, 1971; Virginia, July 8, 1971; Wyoming, July 8, 1971; Georgia, October 4, 1971.

^{xix} This purported amendment was proposed by Congress on September 25, 1789, when it passed the Senate, having previously passed the House on September 24. (1 Annals of Congress 88, 913). It appears officially in 1 Stat. 97. Having received in 1789-1791 only six state ratifications, the proposal then failed of ratification while ten of the 12 sent to the States by Congress were ratified and proclaimed and became the Bill of Rights. The provision was proclaimed as having been ratified and having become the 27th Amendment, when Michigan ratified on May 7, 1992, there being 50 States in the Union. Proclamation was by the Archivist of the United States, pursuant to 1 U.S.C. Sec. 106b, on May 19, 1992. F.R.Doc. 92-11951, 57 Fed. Reg. 21187. It was also proclaimed by votes of the Senate and House of Representatives. 138 Cong. Rec. (daily ed) S 6948-49, H 3505-06.

The several state legislatures ratified the proposal on the following dates: Maryland, December 19, 1789; North Carolina, December 22, 1789; South Carolina, January 19, 1790; Delaware, January 28, 1790; Vermont, November 3, 1791; Virginia, December 15, 1791; Ohio, May 6, 1873; Wyoming, March 6, 1978; Maine, April 27, 1983; Colorado, April 22, 1984; South Dakota, February 1985; New Hampshire, March 7, 1985; Arizona, April 3, 1985; Tennessee, May 28, 1985; Oklahoma, July 10, 1985; New Mexico, February 14, 1986; Indiana, February 24, 1986; Utah, February 25, 1986; Arkansas, March 13, 1987; Montana, March 17, 1987; Connecticut, May 13, 1987; Wisconsin, July 15, 1987; Georgia, February 2, 1988; West Virginia, March 10, 1988; Louisiana, July 7, 1988; Iowa, February 9, 1989; Idaho, March 23, 1989; Nevada, April 26, 1989; Alaska, May 6, 1989; Oregon, May 19, 1989; Minnesota, May 22, 1989; Texas, May 25, 1989; Kansas, April 5, 1990; Florida, May 31, 1990; North Dakota, Mary 25, 1991; Alabama, May 5, 1992; Missouri, May 5, 1992; Michigan, May 7, 1992. New Jersey subsequently ratified on May 7, 1992.

APPENDIX 3

THOMAS JEFFERSON'S LETTER TO THE DANBURY BAPTISTS

The letter from the Danbury Baptist Association[xx] in the State of Connecticut assembled October 7, 1801:

To Thomas Jefferson, Esq.,
President of the United States of America

Sir,

Among the many millions in America and Europe who rejoice in your election to office, we embrace the first opportunity which we have enjoyed in our collective capacity, since your inauguration, to express our great satisfaction in your appointment to the Chief Magistracy in the Unite States. And though the mode of expression may be less courtly and pompous than what many others clothe their addresses with, we beg you, sir, to believe, that none is more sincere.

Our sentiments are uniformly on the side of religious liberty: that Religion is at all times and places a matter between God and individuals, that no man ought to suffer in name, person, or effects on account of his religious opinions, [and] that the legitimate power of civil government extends no further than to punish the man who works ill to his neighbor. But sir, our constitution of government is not specific. Our ancient charter, together with the laws made coincident therewith, were adopted as the basis of our government at the time of our revolution. And such has been our laws and usages, and such still are, [so] that Religion is considered as the first object of Legislation, and therefore what religious privileges we enjoy (as a minor part of the State) we enjoy as favors granted, and not as inalienable rights. And these favors we receive at the expense of such degrading acknowledgments, as are inconsistent with the rights of freemen. It is not to be wondered at therefore, if those who seek after power and gain, under the pretense of government and Religion, should reproach their fellow men, [or] should reproach their Chief Magistrate, as an enemy of religion, law, and good order, because he will not, dares not, assume the prerogative of Jehovah and make laws to govern the Kingdom of Christ.

Sir, we are sensible that the President of the United States is not the National Legislator and also sensible that the national government cannot destroy the laws of each State, but our hopes are strong that the sentiment of our beloved President, which have had such genial effect already, like the radiant beams of the sun, will shine and prevail through all these States—and all the world—until hierarchy and tyranny be destroyed from the earth. Sir, when we reflect on your past services, and see a glow of philanthropy and goodwill shining forth in a course of more than thirty years, we have reason to believe that America's God has raised you up to fill the Chair of State out of that goodwill which he bears to the millions which you preside over. May God strengthen you for the arduous task which providence and the voice of the people have called you—to sustain and support you and your Administration against all the predetermined opposition of those who wish to rise to wealth and importance on the poverty and subjection of the people.

And may the Lord preserve you safe from every evil and bring you at last to his Heavenly Kingdom through Jesus Christ our Glorious Mediator.

Signed in behalf of the Association,

Nehemiah Dodge
Ephraim Robbins
Stephen S. Nelson

Jefferson's Reply: [xxi]

Messrs. Nehemiah Dodge, Ephraim Robbins, and Stephen S. Nelson, A Committee of the Danbury Baptist Association, in the State of Connecticut.

Gentlemen,

The affectionate sentiment of esteem and approbation which you are so good as to express towards me, on behalf of the Danbury Baptist Association, give me the highest satisfaction. My duties dictate a faithful and zealous pursuit of the interests of my constituents, and in proportion as they are persuaded of my fidelity to those duties, the discharge of them becomes more and more pleasing.

Believing with you that religion is a matter which lies solely between man and his God, that he owes account to none other for his faith or his worship, that the legislative powers of government reach actions only, and not opinions, I contemplate with sovereign reverence that act of the whole American people which declared that their legislature would "make no law respecting an establishment of religion, or prohibiting the free exercise thereof," thus building a wall of separation between Church and State. Adhering to this expression of the supreme will of the nation in behalf of the rights of conscience, I shall see with sincere satisfaction the progress of those sentiments which tend to restore to man all his natural rights, convinced he has no natural right in opposition to his social duties.

I reciprocate your kind prayers for the protection and blessing of the common Father and Creator of man, and tender you for yourselves and your religious association, assurances of my high respect and esteem.

/s Thomas Jefferson
Jan. 1, 1802

An actual draft of Jefferson's letter follows as provided by the Library of Congress.

[xx] *Letter of Oct. 7, 1801 from Danbury (CT) Baptist Assoc. to Thomas Jefferson, in Thomas Jefferson Papers, Manuscript Division, Library of Congress, Wash. D.C.*

[xxi] *Letter of Thomas Jefferson in The Writings of Thomas Jefferson, Albert E. Bergh, ed. (Washington, D.C.: The Thomas Jefferson Memorial Association of the United States, 1904), Vol. XVI, pp. 281-82.*

To mess. Nehemiah Dodge, Ephraim Robbins, & Stephen S. Nelson a committee of the Danbury Baptist association in the state of Connecticut.

Gentlemen

The affectionate sentiments of esteem & approbation which you are good as to express towards me, on behalf of the Danbury Baptist association, give me the highest satisfaction. my duties dictate a faithful & zealous pursuit of the interests of my constituents, and, in proportion as they are persuaded of my fidelity to those duties, the discharge of them becomes more & more pleasing.

Believing with you that religion is a matter which lies solely between man & his god, that he owes account to none other for his faith or his worship, that the legitimate powers of government reach actions only, and not opinions, I contemplate with sovereign reverence that act of the whole American people which declared that their legislature should make no law respecting an establishment of religion, or prohibiting the free exercise thereof, thus building a wall of separation between church and state. [Congress thus inhibited from acts respecting religion, and the Executive authorised only to execute their acts, I have refrained from presenting even occasional performances of devotion, Executive is the legal head of church, but subject here, as religious exercise only to the voluntary regulations and discipline of each respective sect. I shall see with sincere satisfaction the progress of those sentiments which tend to restore to man all his natural rights, convinced he has no natural right in opposition to his social duties.

I reciprocate your kind prayers for the protection and blessing of the common father and creator of man, and tender you for yourselves and your religious association, assurances of my high respect & esteem.

Th Jefferson
Jan. 1. 1802.

20593